120TH OPEN CHAMPIONSHIP
Card of the Old Course

Hole	Par	Yards	Hole	Par	Yards
1	4	448	10	4	395
2	4	417	11	4	409
3	4	409	12	3	184
4	3	203	13	4	475
5	4	346	14	3	199
6	4	473	15	5	543
7	3	156	16	4	414
8	4	458	17	5	525
9	4	414	18	4	472
Out	34	3,324	In	36	3,616
			Total	70	6,940

THE OPEN CHAMPIONSHIP 1991

Wife Jennie and Ian Baker-Finch celebrated his victory alongside the eighteenth green.

THE OPEN CHAMPIONSHIP 1991

WRITERS

JOHN HOPKINS
RAYMOND JACOBS
RENTON LAIDLAW
MICHAEL McDONNELL
ALISTER NICOL
MARINO PARASCENZO
MICHAEL WILLIAMS

PHOTOGRAPHERS

LAWRENCE LEVY
BRIAN MORGAN
RUSTY JARRETT

EDITOR

BEV NORWOOD

AUTHORISED BY THE
CHAMPIONSHIP COMMITTEE
OF THE ROYAL AND ANCIENT
GOLF CLUB OF ST ANDREWS

TRANSWORLD PUBLISHERS LTD
61-63 Uxbridge Road, London W5 5SA

TRANSWORLD PUBLISHERS (AUSTRALIA) PTY LTD
15-23 Helles Avenue, Moorebank, NSW 2170

TRANSWORLD PUBLISHERS (NZ) LTD
Cnr Moselle and Waipareira Aves,
Henderson, Auckland

Published 1991 by Partridge Press
a division of Transworld Publishers Ltd

Statistics of 120th Open Championship produced on a
Unisys Computer System.

Photograph on p.23 courtesy of Bob Thomas.
Photograph on p.26 courtesy of Dave Cannon.

A CIP catalogue record for this book is available
from the British Library

1 85225 1131

Phototypeset by Falcon Graphic Art Ltd
Printed in Great Britain
by Richard Clay Ltd, Bungay

CONTENTS

A panoramic view of the fourteenth hole, as Payne Stewart plays on the second day.

THE CHAMPIONSHIP COMMITTEE

CHAIRMAN

G. M. SIMMERS, OBE

DEPUTY CHAIRMAN

H.M. CAMPBELL

COMMITTEE

M. VANS AGNEW
A. R. COLE-HAMILTON
J. C. DAWSON
R. FOSTER
P. W. J. GREENHOUGH
D. I. PEPPER
W. G. N. ROACH
J. K. TATE
P. M. G. UNSWORTH
W. J. UZIELLI

BUSINESS MEMBER

N. J. CRICHTON

ADDITIONAL MEMBER

J. R. VAUGHAN-EVANS
COUNCIL OF NATIONAL GOLF UNIONS

SECRETARY

M. F. BONALLACK, OBE

DEPUTY SECRETARY

W. G. WILSON

CHAMPIONSHIP SECRETARY

D. HILL

ASSISTANT SECRETARY (CHAMPIONSHIPS)

D. R. WEIR

INTRODUCTION

BY G. M. SIMMERS
Chairman of Championship Committee
Royal and Ancient Golf Club of St Andrews

Following two benign Open Championships at Royal Troon and St Andrews, the weather conditions, certainly during the first two days, presented the players with a stiffer test of golf over the links at Royal Birkdale. As a result, there was a record number of 113 competitors qualifying for the final two rounds, all within ten shots of the leader.

Out of this pack emerged a very worthy and popular winner, Ian Baker-Finch, who, leading the field after the third day, completed the first nine holes of the final round in twenty-nine strokes, thereby setting the seal on his first major championship victory.

After his fine performances at St Andrews in 1984 and last year, his win was fully deserved, and we congratulate him and his fellow competitors for their high standard of sportsmanship and for some marvellous golf.

The Championship Committee is pleased to present this official annual, and I hope it will bring back memories to all who attended.

I am most grateful to the literally thousands of volunteer helpers for their tremendous contributions throughout the week and, in particular, to the members of Royal Birkdale Golf Club who so graciously allowed us the courtesy of their famous course.

Finally, as always, I would like to thank all our contributors and photographers for an expert and lasting record of the 120th Open Championship.

G. M. Simmers, OBE

Ian Baker-Finch equalled an Open Championship record with his 130 aggregate for the last two rounds.

FOREWORD

BY IAN BAKER-FINCH

The Open Championship is the most special event of the year in golf. Just to play in it is a thrill, and to win it is a dream. I was in a dream world when I was presented with that famous claret jug at Royal Birkdale.

There were other Sunday afternoons when I had chances to win and did not make it, and the memories of those times made me stronger and more determined to achieve it.

In 1984, I was just a kid with starry eyes having a great time. That Open Championship was the start to my career. People got to know my name. Despite what happened, I couldn't wait to get back.

Last year, I was a bigger kid and learned a lot from the guy who won, Nick Faldo. I have improved since then, and I have a lot to thank Nick for . . . just watching him go on and win, and the way he went about it.

I am sure everyone who wins a major championship thinks it is going to be the first of many, and I certainly hope so. My wife, Jennie, daughter Hayley, and I have many cherished memories of Royal Birkdale, and this book will be a great memento of those days.

Ian Baker-Finch

120TH OPEN CHAMPIONSHIP

* Denotes amateurs

NAME	SCORES				TOTAL	MONEY
Ian Baker-Finch, Australia	71	71	64	66	272	£90,000
Mike Harwood, Australia	68	70	69	67	274	70,000
Fred Couples, USA	72	69	70	64	275	55,000
Mark O'Meara, USA	71	68	67	69	275	55,000
Jodie Mudd, USA	72	70	72	63	277	34,166
Bob Tway, USA	75	66	70	66	277	34,166
Eamonn Darcy, Ireland	73	68	66	70	277	34,166
Craig Parry, Australia	71	70	69	68	278	27,500
Greg Norman, Australia	74	68	71	66	279	22,833
Bernhard Langer, Germany	71	71	70	67	279	22,833
Seve Ballesteros, Spain	66	73	69	71	279	22,833
Rodger Davis, Australia	70	71	73	66	280	17,100
Magnus Sunesson, Sweden	72	73	68	67	280	17,100
David Williams, England	74	71	68	67	280	17,100
Roger Chapman, England	74	66	71	69	280	17,100
Vijay Singh, Fiji	71	69	69	71	280	17,100
Chip Beck, USA	67	78	70	66	281	10,055
Lee Trevino, USA	71	72	71	67	281	10,055
Nick Faldo, England	68	75	70	68	281	10,055
Peter Senior, Australia	74	67	71	69	281	10,055
Paul Broadhurst, England	71	73	68	69	281	10,055
Barry Lane, England	68	72	71	70	281	10,055
Ian Woosnam, Wales	70	72	69	70	281	10,055
Andrew Sherborne, England	73	70	68	70	281	10,055
Mark Mouland, Wales	68	74	68	71	281	10,055
Tom Watson, USA	69	72	72	69	282	6,750
Wayne Grady, Australia	69	70	73	70	282	6,750
Colin Montgomerie, Scotland	71	69	71	71	282	6,750
Eduardo Romero, Argentina	70	73	68	71	282	6,750
Mark James, England	72	68	70	72	282	6,750
Mike Reid, USA	68	71	70	73	282	6,750
Steven Richardson, England	74	70	72	67	283	5,633
Payne Stewart, USA	72	72	71	68	283	5,633
Christy O'Connor, Jr., Ireland	72	71	71	69	283	5,633
Mike Miller, Scotland	73	74	67	69	283	5,633
Gordon Brand, Jr., Scotland	71	72	69	71	283	5,633
Gary Hallberg, USA	68	70	73	72	283	5,633
Anders Forsbrand, Sweden	71	72	73	68	284	4,980
*Jim Payne, England	72	72	70	70	284	–
Nolan Henke, USA	77	71	66	70	284	4,980
Peter O'Malley, Australia	72	71	70	71	284	4,980
Curtis Strange, USA	70	73	69	72	284	4,980
Martin Poxon, England	71	72	67	74	284	4,980
Sam Torrance, Scotland	72	76	70	67	285	4,234
Des Smyth, Ireland	71	73	73	68	285	4,234
Tom Kite, USA	77	71	68	69	285	4,234
Steve Elkington, Australia	71	68	76	70	285	4,234
Robert Gamez, USA	71	72	72	70	285	4,234
Nick Price, Zimbabwe	69	72	73	71	285	4,234
Graham Marsh, Australia	69	73	72	71	285	4,234
Jack Nicklaus, USA	70	75	69	71	285	4,234
Fulton Allem, South Africa	70	72	71	72	285	4,234
Jamie Spence, England	70	73	70	72	285	4,234
David Love III, USA	71	72	69	73	285	4,234
Donnie Hammond, USA	70	75	67	73	285	4,234
Costantino Rocca, Italy	68	73	70	74	285	4,234
Gavin Levenson, South Africa	72	73	73	68	286	3,550
Hale Irwin, USA	74	70	73	69	286	3,550
Tim Simpson, USA	72	72	72	70	286	3,550
Scott Simpson, USA	74	72	70	70	286	3,550
Gary Player, South Africa	75	71	69	71	286	3,550
Jose Rivero, Spain	74	73	68	71	286	3,550
Andrew Magee, USA	71	74	69	72	286	3,550

Gil Morgan, USA	72	74	74	67	287	3,155
Jay Don Blake, USA	75	73	72	67	287	3,155
Steve Pate, USA	73	72	74	68	287	3,155
Michael McLean, England	71	75	72	69	287	3,155
Steve Jones, USA	70	77	71	69	287	3,155
Miguel Martin, Spain	71	75	71	70	287	3,155
Mark McNulty, Zimbabwe	76	71	70	70	287	3,155
Andrew Oldcorn, England	71	67	77	72	287	3,155
Darren Clarke, Ireland	79	67	68	73	287	3,155
Frank Nobilo, New Zealand	74	74	71	69	288	3,000
*Phil Mickelson, USA	77	67	73	71	288	–
Lanny Wadkins, USA	71	75	71	71	288	3,000
Martin Gates, England	67	75	73	73	288	3,000
Peter Jacobsen, USA	75	72	68	73	288	3,000
Tony Johnstone, Zimbabwe	69	74	71	74	288	3,000
Brett Ogle, Australia	73	75	66	74	288	3,000
Miguel A. Jimenez, Spain	74	74	72	69	289	3,000
Fuzzy Zoeller, USA	72	72	75	70	289	3,000
Daniel Silva, Portugal	73	71	75	70	289	3,000
Malcolm Mackenzie, England	71	73	74	71	289	3,000
Ben Crenshaw, USA	71	75	72	71	289	3,000
John Bland, South Africa	71	76	71	71	289	3,000
Mark Brooks, USA	73	74	70	72	289	3,000
Santiago Luna, Spain	67	77	72	73	289	3,000
Danny Mijovic, Canada	70	72	74	73	289	3,000
Jose Maria Olazabal, Spain	74	67	74	74	289	3,000
Howard Clark, England	71	69	73	76	289	3,000
David Gilford, England	72	67	73	77	289	3,000
Brian Marchbank, Scotland	72	73	75	70	290	3,000
Rick Gibson, Canada	73	75	70	72	290	3,000
Peter Teravainen, USA	71	72	72	75	290	3,000
Patrick Hall, England	77	71	72	71	291	3,000
John Hoskison, England	74	73	74	71	292	3,000
Peter Hedblom, Sweden	74	74	73	71	292	3,000
Alastair Webster, England	73	74	73	72	292	3,000
Peter Allan, England	70	71	75	76	292	3,000
Carl Suneson, England	69	77	69	77	292	3,000
Chris Moody, England	74	71	78	71	294	3,000
Magnus Persson, Sweden	77	71	74	72	294	3,000
Craig Stadler, USA	77	71	74	72	294	3,000
John Morse, USA	73	71	77	73	294	3,000
Tom Weiskopf, USA	74	74	73	73	294	3,000
Jeff Sluman, USA	71	71	75	77	294	3,000
Stephen McAllister, Scotland	79	69	70	77	295	3,000
Robin Mann, England	73	74	75	75	297	3,000
Eoghan O'Connell, Ireland	74	74	74	75	297	3,000
John Oates, England	77	71	76	75	299	3,000
Paul Mayo, Wales	71	74	71	83	299	3,000
Neal Briggs, England	73	74	77	76	300	3,000
Richard Boxall, England	71	69	–	–	Retired	

NON QUALIFIERS AFTER 36 HOLES
(All professionals receive £600)

Corey Pavin, USA	74	75	149
Tony Charnley, England	75	74	149
*Robert Allenby, Australia	73	76	149
Kenny Perry, USA	73	76	149
Jose Maria Canizares, Spain	77	73	150
James Heggarty, N. Ireland	74	76	150
Larry Mize, USA	75	75	150
Philip Walton, Ireland	74	76	150
David Frost, South Africa	76	74	150
Simon Townend, England	78	72	150
John Hawksworth, England	77	73	150
Marc Farry, France	75	75	150
Mats Lanner, Sweden	75	75	150
Mark Calcavecchia, USA	71	79	150
Jim Rutledge, Canada	74	76	150
Adam Hunter, Scotland	75	75	150
Jean Van de Velde, France	73	77	150
Masahiro Kuramoto, Japan	71	80	151
Rocco Mediate, USA	76	75	151
*Henry Roblin, England	71	80	151
Peter Smith, Scotland	78	74	152
Lucien Tinkler, Belgium	75	77	152
Ricky Kawagishi, Japan	71	81	152
Greg Turner, New Zealand	77	75	152
*Andrew Coltart, Scotland	73	80	153
David Graham, Australia	75	78	153
Yago Beamonte, Spain	72	81	153
*Gary Evans, England	77	76	153
Glyn Krause, England	75	78	153
Manuel Pinero, Spain	79	74	153
Sandy Stephen, Scotland	75	79	154
*Rolf Muntz, Netherlands	75	79	154
Johnny Miller, USA	74	80	154
Miguel Fernandez, Argentina	81	73	154
David Feherty, N. Ireland	79	75	154
*Jonathan Wilshire, England	76	79	155
Fredrik Lindgren, Sweden	79	76	155
Mark Roe, England	73	82	155
Mikael Hogberg, Sweden	78	78	156
Craig Corrigan, England	76	80	156
Raymond Floyd, USA	80	78	158
Ronald M Gregan, Scotland	79	87	166
Sandy Lyle, Scotland	79	NR	

Ian Baker-Finch strokes the final putt, with the crowd surrounding the eighteenth hole at Royal Birkdale.

ROUND ROYAL BIRKDALE

No. 1 448 Yards, Par 4

The ridge short and right of the green was reduced in height in time for the 1983 Open Championship, so that players who drove down that side of the fairway could have a clearer view of the flagstick. Still, jointly with the eighteenth, this was the most difficult hole on the last day eight years ago.

No. 2 417 Yards, Par 4

The introduction to Birkdale's pre-eminent feature – the fairway, slightly obscured from the tee, leading to a green set below encircling sandhills. The defences of the target area are strongly reinforced by bunkers.

No. 3 409 Yards, Par 4

Again, in an accommodating wind, or even none at all, another chance to hedge bets against future problems. Since a spur of dune to the right of the green may prevent a view of the ultimate target, the tee shot should be held to the left side of the fairway.

No. 4 203 Yards, Par 3

The first hole on the course to have been significantly altered since the Open was last here. The target from the elevated tee has been moved slightly to the left, the green itself is less flat than before, and a new bunker has been introduced.

No. 5 346 Yards, Par 4

Another realistic hope for a birdie. To establish a positive pitch from the elbow of the fairway, as it swings gently to the right, an iron club from the tee is the probable choice. But to be on the 'right' side of the hole is essential, since the green slopes sharply from the back towards the player.

No. 6 473 Yards, Par 4

Rumours of the exacting nature of this hole proved, at least in the final round eight years ago, to be somewhat exaggerated, but this may yet be a hole to be feared. The average score in 1983 among the sixty-three qualifiers matched its par exactly.

No. 7 156 Yards, Par 3

A new tee, first used in the Amateur Championship two years ago, comes into play, from the same lofty eminence but to the left of the previous launching pad. Two bunkers have been added to tighten up the defences of the green, where there are now more options for the examiners to set questions of pin placement hitherto denied to them.

No. 8 458 Yards, Par 4

Arguably the best hole of them all. The drive is from an elevated tee to a fairway curving gradually left, where sandhills lurk to balance the bunkers and ditches opposite. The green is raised between bunkers, almost certainly demanding more club than meets the eye.

No. 9 414 Yards, Par 4

The drive is blind to a hog's back of a fairway, which has marginally more trouble to its left, the more desirable line, than to the right. The green sits above a valley and here again adequate clubbing for the second shot is essential.

No. 10 395 Yards, Par 4

One of Birkdale's most attractive, as well as challenging, holes, despite its modest length. The fairway swings sharply to the left, forcing the drive away from the willow scrub but towards bunkers to the right. From there the approach is to a green sloping sharply.

No. 11 409 Yards, Par 4

That most alarming of prospects, a two-shot hole, dead straight and with the targets of fairway and green unequivocally defined. More trouble left than right and, although the second shot is straightforward enough, getting close to the hole on a particularly expansive green to make less than par is seldom easy.

No. 12 184 Yards, Par 3

Birkdale's benchmark, high dunes, flank the target, which is defended by bunkers short of the green. Severe trouble also lies in wait for the overhit shot, so the sanctuary of the green is all the more welcome at a hole ranked third for difficulty.

No. 13 475 Yards, Par 4

Another significant change from eight years ago. The tee has been moved forward to convert the hole from what had become a purely notional par five into a two-shotter of strength and merit. A ditch lies to the left and the two bunkers by the green (out of ten in all) have been extended to narrow the entrance.

No. 14 199 Yards, Par 3

The green, although as tightly-bunkered as any, is larger than most at Birkdale. Accordingly, it may be more accessible, but from the elevated tee club selection becomes all the more important as the best way of avoiding the anti-climax of taking three putts.

No. 15 543 Yards, Par 5

Especially into the wind, a fearsome prospect. If the drive has successfully avoided bunkers and scrub, there remains as obstacles to the second shot, a selection of eight bunkers strategically ranged to catch the truant ball. A par will seem like a birdie.

No. 16 414 Yards, Par 4

The tee has been raised so as to grant a less obscure view of the fairway. On the right of it is the plaque commemorating Arnold Palmer's amazing recovery in the last round of the 1961 Open Championship, from a small bush through a fierce wind on to a pulpit green above four bunkers.

No. 17 525 Yards, Par 5

The bunkering beside the green has, like that at the thirteenth, been revised so as to tighten the entrance to the target area and make the second shot more exacting at a hole which also had become among the least difficult on the course.

No. 18 472 Yards, Par 4

The player needing a four here to win will, as usual, be thoroughly tested – both in nerve and shot-making. The most desirable route to shorten the second shot involves a carry over a bunker of some 230 yards. Out of bounds lurks down the right side and a substantial, well-bunkered green will search out the second shot.

BIRKDALE OFFERS WELL-DEFINED TARGETS

BY RAYMOND JACOBS

Royal Birkdale Golf Club, before it graduated to regality and then to celebrity, perhaps unwittingly had already established a niche for itself. On 30 July 1889, nine gentlemen, apparently not one of them a Scot, assembled in a private house to form what would become a famous golfing fraternity and, politically correct before its time, sorority.

A sense of obligation to conform was expressed in an original course of nine holes (cost £5.50), the appointment of a professional (60 pence per week), and an overspend on the budget of 81 pence. The course was later extended to eighteen holes.

A wooden clubhouse was built by the present fourth green in 1904 but was demolished in 1933, when the links were radically redesigned. The somewhat clinical appearance of the replacement building was variously described as resembling a battleship or as an example of early airport terminal architecture. 'What say they? Let them say,' would be the repeatable interpretation of the members' response.

The golf course was redesigned by Fred Hawtree and J. H. Taylor, the Open champion five times. They made six new holes, built five new greens to existing holes, redesigned four greens, and added twenty new tees and five new fairways. The modifications cost £4,000. Their concept, which has been amended over the years, was for the holes to follow the line of the valleys between the sandhills rather than over them. Each hole was self-contained. Blind shots were almost entirely eliminated. From flat fairways, the greens set into the dunes became targets as well-defined as they are at Muirfield. If the result was a certain degree of sameness in the holes, their fairness could not be contested.

Over the years, many alterations have been carried out, basically in acknowledgement of the increasing distances players hit the ball, and to ease crowd movement and control, but the intrinsic difficulties have been unchanged. There is the ample bunkering and, most punishing of all, Birkdale's benchmark hazards, the buckthorn and willow scrub. When the towering dunes were added, which provided vantage points outside the gallery ropes, if not always easily scaled, the overall effect was to give what the leading American architect, Robert Trent Jones, Jr., described as his profession's primary design goal – natural definition.

Birkdale had been in existence only twenty years when the club became host to its first event of national consequence, the British women's championship. Since then every golfing occasion of distinction has been held at Birkdale – Ryder Cup, Walker Cup and Curtis Cup matches, numerous professional tournaments, and British and English amateur championships. In Ronnie White and Frances Smith, Birkdale has produced two of Britain's foremost postwar amateurs. The Open Championship was a latecomer, but a fourteen-year delay was by fate rather than by design.

The Open Championship was to have been played here in the summer of 1940, but by then, of course, the Second World War was underway. The previous year the club had celebrated its fiftieth anniversary and a commemorative booklet ended with the words: 'In 1940 (the club) will reach the highest triumph of all when it is the venue for the British Open – regarded in every country where golf is played as the championship of the world.' When the Open finally came to Birkdale in 1954 the club had been Royal Birkdale for three years, the title bestowed by King George VI, perhaps the last member of the Royal Family to take to golf seriously until the recent reports of the active interest in the game shown by the Duke of York.

The dunes which frame the fairways are a prominent characteristic. Arnold Palmer's famous shot (inset) is commemorated.

ARNOLD PALMER
THE OPEN CHAMPIONSHIP
14TH JULY 1961

If Ben Hogan's decision not to defend the title at Royal Birkdale after his emphatic victory at Carnoustie was a disappointment, the merit of Peter Thomson's triumph was undeniable. Its significance would, moreover, only later become clear. Having finished second in the two previous Opens, Thomson won what was to be the first of three Opens in succession, the first time that had been accomplished since Bob Ferguson had done it in 1880–82. Thomson – detached, always seeming to play within himself, the thinking man's golfer – was the first Australian to win the title, and he set the precedent that no British or European player would win in six, now seven, attempts over these links.

A par at the last hole by Dai Rees would have set Thomson a target score of 283; instead the Welshman's second shot scampered through the green and he missed for his four from five feet. Thomson could take five and win with a 283 aggregate. Having bunkered his second, Thomson did just that, allowing himself what must have seemed the hazardous liberty of making the winning stroke with the back of his putter. Poor Rees. He led, alone or jointly, after the third round of the Open Championship five times, yet was never better than second – which, by an unhappy coincidence for him, he was again at Birkdale seven years later.

Under the Commonwealth domination of Thomson and South African, Bobby Locke – each won four times in the ten years from 1949 – the Open could not fairly be described as 'the championship of the world'. The importance of Arnold Palmer's victory in 1961, especially after his narrow defeat by Kel Nagle the year before, was to revive interest in the event among America's leading professionals, and re-establish its status as the most international of the major championships. Yet, appalling conditions almost sabotaged the championship and challenged Palmer's passion to win it. The first day's weather was mixed but manageable, the lull before the storm on Thursday, when a ferocious wind laid waste the tented area. A torrential rain then caused Friday's play (two rounds then) to be postponed.

In the first round there were only four scores below 70, and the leading twenty-four finishers played the second round in a total of 130 strokes more than in the first round. Palmer's opening 73 included five birdies in the first six holes and only eleven putts on the outward half. Before Palmer could be sure of winning he had to accept a penalty stroke when, seen only by himself, the ball moved in a bunker. He also had to make two stunning recoveries for par and withstand a brave counter-attack by Rees who, four strokes behind with five holes to play, finished birdie, birdie, par, birdie. British audiences became aware of the stamp of Palmer's game: his extraordinary capacity for bringing off the shot full of calculated risk.

By the time the Open returned to Birkdale in 1965, the trans-Atlantic interest had been fully rekindled. The championship was both nostalgic and innovative. It was the last time that the final two rounds were played on the same day, a Friday. Tony Lema defended, and a wealth of leading US and other overseas players entered. The race, however, once more went to the smart. Peter Thomson – now aged thirty-five, but who had not lost the cutting edge of his ambition – again mastered a running course with accuracy and judgement to join James Braid and J. H. Taylor as winners of the title five times. Not since Henry Cotton's victory at Carnoustie in 1937, opposed by the members of the US Ryder Cup team, had an overseas invasion been so resolutely repulsed.

Lema, who was killed in an air crash a year later, defended so stoutly, that on the seventeenth tee in the final round his target for victory was 4,4 against Thomson's 4,5. Lema bogeyed both holes and Thomson went 4,4 – reaching the last two greens with a driver and three iron 'perfectly struck and impeccably straight', as a contemporary account put it. Thomson's most satisfying win did not come easily, considering that Thomson was six strokes behind Lema after the first round and had a three-stroke lead with nine holes to play in the final round reduced to one stroke after he had missed putts of six, two, nine and four feet on the next four greens.

Six years later, Lee Trevino had emerged from a golfing background far removed from the country club, college-coached ranks out of which the most talented American players usually emerge. Victory in the US Open three years before, and in regular tournaments since, had marked him out as a likely winner. The flat, thrusting swing from a pronounced open stance brought from Trevino the analysis: 'You can talk to a fade, but a hook won't listen.' The method proved so eminently adaptable that, within the space of a month, Trevino not only regained the US Open title, but added the Canadian Open and, for the first time, the Open Championship.

This was the 100th Open, the centenary edition having been celebrated at St Andrews eleven years before, and Trevino marked the occasion by becoming only the fourth player – after Bobby Jones, Gene Sarazen and Ben Hogan – to win the British and US titles in the same summer, an achievement matched in 1982 by Tom Watson. In the event, Trevino almost threw away entirely the advantage of three strokes he held with only two holes to play. The sandhills and rough at the seventeenth cost him seven, but Lu Liang Huan, of Taiwan, the first Asian to make an impact on the championship, could do no better than reduce Trevino's advantage to one, and that slender margin was enough for Trevino to steal home for the first of successive wins.

The next two Opens to come to Birkdale, in 1976 and 1983, had two elements in common – hot weather and the emergence of a young player who would develop into a championship winner. Severiano Ballesteros was the first, and Nick Faldo, the second, and their subsequent exploits more than confirmed the expectations they raised. The progress made by the Continental, as distinct from British, professionals to the strength they have now, can be dated to the cavalier performance of the Spaniard, then an unranked nineteen year old. Indeed, Ballesteros, by tieing for second place with Jack Nicklaus, even though six strokes behind Johnny Miller, could be seen in hindsight as lending further impetus to the Open's stature.

On a parched links, whose mottled greens putted better than they looked, Ballesteros led by three strokes from Miller with seventeen holes to play. Thereafter, however, Miller, one of the most fearless shot-makers and ruthless scorers the game has known, was in command. There were three two-stroke swings to Miller, and when at the eleventh Ballesteros hooked disastrously into the dreaded scrub, took four to reach the green, and added three putts, Miller's four effectively resolved the issue. Ballesteros' naïve golf was evident neither in the eagle he made at the seventeenth nor in the memorable chip-and-run between two bunkers by the home green to four feet. Miller's 66 was the lowest last round by a winner, a record which lasted all of twelve months until Watson beat it by a stroke in his titanic duel with Nicklaus at Turnberry.

Seven years on, and the course, after rain in the spring and early summer was followed by a prolonged period of hot weather, was more grassed than was desirable for a links. In these 'trans-Atlantic' conditions, scoring records were set: the average of the first ten players to finish, 69.58; the qualifying total after the second and third rounds, 146 and 217; Craig Stadler's opening score, 64; and Denis Durnian's outward half in the second round, 28, six under par. On the other hand, Hale Irwin whiffed a two-inch putt at the fourteenth in the third round and ultimately finished second equal with Andy Bean, a stroke behind Watson, who joined James Braid, J. H. Taylor and Thomson in gaining his fifth victory – in only nine attempts and for the first time in England.

But for Faldo, as with Ballesteros, the very experience of being in contention was to prove important. Although he began the championship 6,6 – to be instantly six over par – Faldo was tied for the lead with only seven holes to play. He then bogeyed the twelfth, and took three putts at the thirteenth and fourteenth, before dropping another stroke at the sixteenth to finish joint eighth. Watson, needing a four at the last to win, hit a superb two iron safely home from 213 yards out, a shot very similar to the one with which Thomson had secured his fifth victory eighteen years before. Royal Birkdale, after six Open Championships – variously memorable, was left waiting for its first winner from Europe.

Twenty years after his victory here, Lee Trevino was still entertaining the crowds at Royal Birkdale.

PUTTING A SMILE ON GOLF

BY MICHAEL McDONNELL

It is an enduring and defining quality of the great golf champions that each bestows some unmistakable facet upon the game, and in so doing, offers testimony to his own time and personal style.

In times past, golf was given a certain flamboyance by Walter Hagen, an elegance by Sir Henry Cotton. In more modern times, it gathered pace and excitement from a breathtaking Arnold Palmer; acquired towering importance from the inexhaustible excellence of Jack Nicklaus; and a spiritual depth from the little South African Gary Player, for whom golf was always part of a wider mission.

But it was the grandson of a Mexican grave-digger who was to bestow perhaps the most cherished gift of all. Lee Buck Trevino put a smile on the face of golf. He gave it laughter. More than that, he brought a sense of joy and proportion to a pursuit that had always been in danger of taking itself too seriously.

Yet his historical importance extends beyond a mere theatrical ability to entertain a public while making superlative golf look surprisingly easy. The Era of Trevino stands as a period when the royal and ancient game broadened its appeal to a generation which previously had never considered it as being for the likes of them. It was Trevino who showed them the way.

Quite simply, through the manner of his achievements, he was able to sweep away the myths and some of the prejudices that surrounded the sport, and show it to be not only a game of the people that was not dependent on background, but one which responded solely to the degree of enthusiasm with which it was approached.

Lee Trevino, on his own admission, came from the other side of the tracks in Texas. Indeed his personal pilgrimage to success possesses all the ingredients of the Great American Dream in which a man, no matter how humble his origins, can climb as high as he dares, provided he believes in his own abilities.

Within his chosen vocation, the sudden and unexpected appearance of Super Mex on the threshold of world golf, was to be a milestone in its development. From the start, he demonstrated that it was a game to be enjoyed, and that it could be played to the highest level without losing any of its buoyancy.

There had never been anybody like him; at least anybody who could appear so carefree, yet at the same time perform consistently to the highest standards. He had been self-taught and in the hardest of schools, at times wagering to pay his way. He had even come to the professional game through a circuitous route of occupations, including a stint in the US Marines, because there did not seem much else to do.

This was no prodigy born to the game, for whom all else was brushed aside so that his path to the top

(Previous page) Playfully, Tony Jacklin tried to silence Trevino in 1971, but Lee already had the victory.

could be as straightforward as possible. This man was perilously close to thirty years old before the world heard of him. In a sense he was the outsider who had gate-crashed the party and found himself on the top table.

He was the antithesis of what a champion should be, or rather of what the archetypal champion had been until then. He had a tattoo on his arm in memory of a former love. He displayed an unequivocal disdain for archaic values wherever he found them within the game. In short, he brought a refreshing wind of change to a sport that could not ignore him because of his supreme talent.

Even his golf swing seemed to offer complete defiance of orthodoxy (although clearly it obeyed the appropriate rules of physics to work with remarkable consistency). It was a flat, measured swipe that seemed to halt just safely short of delivering a destructive slice – but only just – and it was matched by a flawless short game and sureness of touch that could only have been acquired through countless money matches, bets and side-bets, whether won or lost.

Yet he possessed such a huge talent that Nicklaus remarked that once Trevino himself realized how good he really was, the rest of them could pack up and go home. What Jack had perceived was a golfing intelligence – an ability to learn and understand – that is the gift of all great players. It is facility to see what is required and then to produce it. Thus, when Trevino first beheld links golf, he seemed perfectly suited to its demands, because not only had he learned to hit low-flying shots to cheat the winds of Texas, but he had the ability to manufacture strokes not found in textbooks.

That said, the secret of success lies in the blend of these technical skills with the common strategies of winning, and in this respect, the learning process for Trevino was to be rather costly. A disastrous last-round 77 during the 1970 Open, when Trevino held the lead, handed over the stage to Nicklaus and Doug Sanders for a play-off. And yet there is another quality common to great golfers – a mistake made is a lesson learned and never happens again.

When Trevino arrived in Southport at what seemed the last minute for the 1971 Open Championship, his chance of success seemed not even worthy of discussion because it was assumed, quite apart from jet lag, he must suffer some reaction from the momentous events in which he had been involved during the previous few weeks.

It had been a busy time which started when he became US Open champion at Merion, beating Nicklaus in a play-off. Two weeks later he had moved to Montreal to become Canadian Open champion by dismissing Art Wall in a play-off. By the time he reached the Lancashire coast, he discovered that most of his main rivals had been hard at preparation for at least two or three days and there was much catching up to be done.

The prize at Merion had been the sweetest, because he let slip an outright chance of victory by missing a putt on the last green after a spectator distracted him, yet still managed to redeem himself in the eighteen-hole play-off. More significantly, he had vanquished Nicklaus, the man he most respected and admired both on and off the fairways.

Nicklaus set the standards by which all of them judged their own games, and Trevino had taken on the Golden Bear head-to-head and contained him. Curiously enough, Nicklaus had proved to be the more tentative, particularly with his wedge play, and may to this day still wince at the memory of his attempted flick to Merion's tenth green, which never reached the putting surface. Even when there had seemed the occasional glimmer of hope for Nicklaus, Trevino had dashed it – as on the fifteenth green, when he holed an outrageous putt even though Nicklaus had been much closer.

But then this was Trevino at his best – when he could see the other man and match him stroke-for-stroke. It was to be much the same in Montreal for the Canadian Open title when, after a week's interlude at an event in Cleveland in which he made little impact, he again found himself squaring up to a rival in a play-off.

This time it was the veteran Wall, then approaching his fiftieth year, who looked as though he would become champion when he stood over a putt on the final green. But the crowd began to move and it took marshals fully fifteen minutes to settle them before he could play the stroke – and miss.

In a sense there was an inevitability about the outcome. Wall had missed his chance of a surprise win and was to be no match for the younger man in the sudden-death play-off, which he lost at the first extra hole.

The most persistent question Trevino faced when he arrived at the Open Championship venue was whether he had left it all rather too late to make the adjustments – time difference, tiredness, links golf, smaller British golf ball, etc. – and he could only reply that they would all have to wait and see.

By the end of two rounds, when he had scored 69 and 70 to join the British hero, Tony Jacklin, at the front of the field, they had their answer. Neither man could have known then how often and crucially their paths were to cross in future years in a rivalry that would eventually see both facing each other as Ryder Cup captains.

That team match was to be the only occasion on which Jacklin would score a personal victory in their face-to-face encounters. In truth, he was to lose much more, and once confessed that it was Trevino who eventually put an end to his championship career because of the manner of the defeats he had inflicted upon him.

Looking back, it was as though Jacklin, who had won the 1969 title and was still at the height of his powers, was destined to be edged out decisively whenever they clashed. On that third day at Royal Birkdale he scored an impressive 67. Not good enough. His playing partner, Trevino, had scored 66 despite some boisterous antics from a partisan crowd.

A year later, when Trevino had chipped on Muirfield's seventeenth green to snatch an Open title Jacklin thought was in his pocket, and then a few months later had defeated him in the World Match Play Championship at Wentworth, the Englishman reflected glumly, 'I can't wait for the year to end.' By his own admission, he was never to be the same competitive force again.

On the final day at Royal Birkdale in 1971, Trevino had been paired with Lu Liang Huan – a Taiwanese professional known affectionately to thousands of British fans as Mister Lu. He had won instant attention for the endearing manner with which he doffed his hat whenever he holed a birdie putt, and demonstrated a miraculous touch.

Moreover, he was to become the chief threat to Trevino's chances, as Jacklin faded on the final day, still at odds with his golf swing. More specifically the other threat to Super Mex's prospects that day was his own disastrous drive from the seventeenth tee when he was comfortably clear of his rival. The ball disappeared high into the towering sandhills on the left-hand side of the fairway.

His first recovery attempt moved the ball only a few yards. His next sent it scurrying across the fairway to the rough on the other side, and he was still not on the green in four strokes. Those who stood there that day sensed the despair of a man who knew he was throwing it all away but could do nothing about it.

What saved him was the simple fact that Mister Lu knew he could not hit the ball far enough to get home with his second shot, and, therefore, would have to rely on a chip and a putt for any hope of a birdie. Under such pressure Mister Lu faltered, and allowed Trevino to walk from that green with a seven on his card but still one stroke ahead.

It was to be enough. Lee Trevino was Open champion. And in his customary style, too. Super Mex never marched inexorably to glory but invariably took a diversion through some last-minute crisis or drama before delivering the goods. So it had been at Royal Birkdale. And Montreal and Merion, too.

His stamina and skill were beyond question. But what he had also demonstrated in those remarkable three weeks which culminated in the events at Birkdale, was an indomitable spirit to keep fighting against the odds. It was a lesson he had learned away from the fairways in his impoverished Texas childhood, and one he brought to golf.

It had made him a champion. Not simply of golf. But of thousands of people who were touched by his personal example, and whose lives were inspired because of him. It was to be the fourth – and perhaps the most important – victory for Lee Buck Trevino in that summer of '71.

A dramatic forty-foot birdie gave Seve Ballesteros the first-round lead with a 66.

DAY

1

THE 1976 OPEN REVISITED

BY MICHAEL WILLIAMS

Everybody remembers 1976. This was the year Johnny Miller won. For once everyone also remembers who was second – Severiano Ballesteros. This was the year when everyone recognized that a new force had been delivered to the game of golf. Here was a raw young man of lithe build, a flashing smile and all the bravado of a Spanish bullfighter; one who knew no fear as he swiped the ball all over the majestic links of Royal Birkdale, climbed sandhills to find it and then swiped it again to distant greens where, again and again, he holed putts for ridiculous birdies or, failing that, got away with pars to which he had little right.

For three days this nineteen year old, who hardly knew a word of English, so much so that every time he was hauled before the world's Press he had to have an interpreter at his side, led the best there was in the game at that time a flamenco of a dance. It was his second Open, not that there had been much to write home about in his first, since he had taken 79 and 80 and made an early departure from Carnoustie, but now here he was scoring a 69 in the first round to share the lead, repeating it in the second to lead on his own by two strokes and following it with a 73 to stay two ahead.

What happened after that was, wise men would have told you at the time, wholly predictable. Ballesteros blew up. He took 38 to the turn, wrecked himself further with a seven at the eleventh and left Miller, American Open champion two years earlier when he had a record final round of 63 at Oakmont, to set another new mark for the Open with a 66 to win by six strokes, the biggest margin for fourteen years.

Ballesteros was second with Jack Nicklaus, but it took a lot of heroics to do it, four birdies in his last six holes, though it has to be borne in mind that in 1976 both the thirteenth and eighteenth holes were par fives, whereas in 1991 they were par fours. Nonetheless that was 4,2,5,4,4,4 and the chip Ballesteros fashioned between the two bunkers to the left of the eighteenth green showed not only the touch, but also the vision of someone with genius in his veins.

And so, in the eyes of the world, if not his family, who had seen it coming for years, a new star was born. As he held the silver claret jug, Miller remarked that it probably had been in the best interest of 'Sevvy', which was the way everyone spelt the abbreviation at the time, that he had not won. 'It would have been too soon to handle all that goes with being an Open champion.'

Seve, as we now spell it, smiled and nodded as if in understanding. In fact, of course, he could not understand a word and, when later it was translated to him, he still could not understand. But, fifteen years on, as the 1991 Open Championship returned to Royal Birkdale, it all came back to him as the draw

(Previous page) Walker Cup player Gary Evans hit the first shot of the Open Championship.

for the first round brought him and Miller out of the hat together again for a re-enactment of those final eighteen holes together. Now, at thirty-four, a man who had seen it all, he knew very well what Miller had meant and he knew he had been right.

It was a time to dwell on how much had changed.

Miller is forty-four, a 'yesterday's man' who probably makes more money building golf courses and doing television commentaries than he ever did as a golfer. Ballesteros, on the other hand, is still around the summit of the game, three Opens and two Masters in his locker and, by the length of one of the drives he now hits with a metal driver, the most popular golfer in Europe.

There had nevertheless been some sign that Ballesteros' star was not shining quite as brightly as it had, even though he had maintained his record of winning at least one tournament in Europe every year since he took the Dutch Open the week after he had finished joint second to Miller in 1976. It had come, therefore, as a relief when, in 1991, Ballesteros came back to life again, winning his first tournament for almost a year, in Japan, and immediately following it with a run in which he lost a play-off for the Spanish Open but took both the Volvo PGA Championship and then the Dunhill Masters. That was three firsts and a second in four attempts.

That was much more like the old Ballesteros, but he also had developed a new theme, and that was to be quite devastating in the first round. Beginning with that Spanish Open at Club de Campo, Ballesteros' first-round scores in Europe read 63, 67, 66, 62, 63 and now here at Royal Birkdale, as he began his assault on the Open Championship, so he maintained that momentum with a 66 to lead the field. It was almost as if it had been pre-ordained: Ballesteros 66, Miller 74 – just as in that last round in 1976 it had been Miller 66, Ballesteros 74.

How the crowds rose to Ballesteros as he finished in a blaze of glory with an eagle-three at the seventeenth and then a birdie at the eighteenth to break a deadlock between Martin Gates, who had gone out amid the dawn patrol at 7.25 a.m.; Chip Beck, the American Ryder Cup player; and Santiago Luna, from Spain, all of whom had 67s.

Only seventeen of the 156-man field broke 70, eight of them teeing off before 10 a.m., which gave some indication of the variable weather. The forecast had been full of foreboding, but the morning turned out to be quite pleasant. Around midday, however, the wind switched into its more traditional westerly quarter and steadily increased in strength, making the golf course a much tougher proposition.

Gates is in his first season on the European Tour. He is based in Jersey, and made one early mark by finishing fourth in the Italian Open. Now, out with the dawn patrol, he set the pace with his 67, followed by Beck ninety minutes later and then Luna, whose 12.25 p.m. starting time meant that he had to battle his way through much the same sort of elements that confronted Ballesteros.

Nick Faldo, the defending champion, was amid a group of seven with 68. Alongside him were two other British players in Barry Lane and Mark Mouland; two Americans in Gary Hallberg and Mike Reid; an Italian, Costantino Rocca; and an Australian, Mike Harwood. Two other Australians, Wayne Grady, the reigning American PGA champion, and Graham Marsh, had 69s, as did Tom Watson, the 1983 champion at Royal Birkdale, two Zimbabweans in Nick Price and Tony Johnstone and a little-known British professional, Carl Suneson.

Eleven players equalled par, among them Ian Woosnam, the Masters champion, and Jack Nicklaus, but it was undoubtedly Ballesteros who stole the thunder with what was for twelve holes in difficult conditions a flawless display. By that time he was two under par, struggling only at the sixth hole, a ferocious par four of 473 yards which by the end of the championship had established itself, in relation to par, as the most severe hole of the lot. It had a scoring average of 4.59 and there were in four days only eighteen birdies as against thirty-eight eagles and 357 birdies at the seventeenth, admittedly a par five. Only the fifteenth, seventy yards longer and very much a par five, played harder with an average of 4.99.

Ballesteros got his par at the sixth with a deft wedge shot from a bank to four feet. He was out in 33, with one birdie at the fifth hole, picked up another at the tenth, and was going as smooth as

Masahiro Kuramoto (top) led the Japanese contingent, while another veteran of the Japan Tour, Australian Graham Marsh (bottom) returned a 69 to be amongst the leaders. American Mike Reid, shaking hands with Marsh, had a 68.

silk. It was, therefore, to his intense annoyance that, after a perfect two-iron shot down the thirteenth, he needed but a gentle nine iron to the green, underhit and did not get down in a chip and single putt. Redressing that with a twenty-foot putt for a two at the fourteenth, Ballesteros was for the only time in his round in trouble as he put his face to the wind on the fifteenth hole. An intended safe two-iron shot from the tee led instead to difficulty, and by the time of his fourth shot he still needed a seven iron to reach the green. He two-putted for a bogey-six. 'It took rather a long time,' he reflected.

However his finish made up for it as, downwind, he reached the seventeenth green with a drive and nine iron to four feet for a straightforward eagle and then negotiated the eighteenth with a four iron from the tee, a seven iron to the green and a putt of forty feet that ran and ran and ran before falling in, to thunderous cheers at its last gasp.

Gates, having qualified at Southport and Ainsdale, was playing in his first Open. That was, he said, his first goal and now his second was to get through all four days, which happily he did. To chip in for a birdie at his first hole was quite a start, and he also holed from twenty feet for a two at the fourth. Only inexperience cost him his first dropped stroke at the ninth. He tried to chip over some television cables, which could have been lifted. His ball hit the cables. Another shot went at the thirteenth.

He quickly dusted himself down with a wonderful finish as he played the last five holes in three under with birdies at the fourteenth, sixteenth and seventeenth to put his name firmly on top of the leaderboard.

Lane looked like joining or even overtaking Gates when he went to five under par for the first eleven holes, but was undone when his one iron from the thirteenth flew so far that it ran into a bunker 310 yards from the tee. It cost him a five. Another shot was dropped at the fourteenth, where he hit through the green, and he got into all manner of trouble at the sixteenth, dropping two shots before he got one of them back at the seventeenth for his 68.

Instead Beck was the first to join Gates, though in reverse circumstances. The man with the best

U.S. Open winner Payne Stewart (left) had six bogeys in his 72, defender Nick Faldo (above) went round in 68, and former American champion Curtis Strange (below) had an uphill struggle to a 70.

(Opposite page) American Chip Beck (left) posted a 67, Masters winner Ian Woosnam (right) had a 70, and Mark Mouland (below) made his best start in the Open with a 68.

American record in the 1989 Ryder Cup match was two over par after four holes but then produced five birdies in his next eleven holes. It was confirmation of his rediscovered form which had begun at the time of the Masters.

Luna, an engaging Spaniard, had some difficulty in recalling how exactly he had made his 67, possibly because he was still in a daze having nearly emulated 'my good friend Seve' by finishing birdie, eagle, bogey, and in almost identical manner. Luna too had faced not much more than a tap-in at the seventeenth and then demolished the 472-yard eighteenth with nothing more than a drive and wedge before taking three putts from forty feet for his five.

A 68 by Faldo on what was his thirty-fourth birthday looked an ominously good start. He was the first to admit that he had the best of the weather, though it was still some time before he found top gear. With dropped shots at the first and sixth holes, relieved by a birdie at the second, he was still one over par with five holes to play. A bold four-iron shot at the fourteenth, held against the right-to-left wind and coming down between the bunker and flag, produced a birdie-two and that got him going. Further birdies at the sixteenth and seventeenth tucked him nicely into position after the first round.

A 72 by Payne Stewart, the American Open champion, was largely the result of his taking too many strokes around the greens, and instead it was Hallberg and Reid who became the standard bearers of the Stars and Stripes. Hallberg had recently got rather caught up in the mechanics of the game, rather than just visualizing the shot and then playing it. Two under par for the first four holes, he was away to a fine start and held it.

Conversely, Reid made his move with an inward half of 33, with three birdies in his last four holes. A man of studious appearance, he loves playing in Britain. 'This is real golf,' he said, 'something we don't have in America. There it is more a form of archery. Here there is a tee and there is a green and you work out how you're going to get from one to the other.'

Watson was far from happy with his short-iron play in his 69, rating it, on a scale of ten, at about

Barry Lane (left) was amongst the leaders with a 68, and Carl Suneson (below left) followed him by one stroke.

Andrew Sherborne (above) escaped with a 73, while Tony Johnstone (below) returned a 69.

three. Nor was he exactly confident on the greens, missing from three feet at the first hole; in due course he did sink a couple of beauties, from thirty-five feet for a three at the ninth and from twenty feet for a two at the thirteenth. Rocca, who was enjoying a fine season on the European Tour, went along with those sentiments, missing three times from inside ten feet, but still getting round in 68.

Woosnam, who had recently acquired his own private plane so that he could commute from his Oswestry home, was never in complete command of his game, especially from the tee. His 70 was about the best he could have hoped to squeeze out of it.

Having been the first reserve after losing a sixteen-hole qualifying sudden-death play-off at Hillside, Jimmy Heggarty got in at very short notice when Ronan Rafferty pulled out on the first tee with a damaged shoulder. Heggarty was so rushed that he hardly knew what day it was for four holes, and he may not have been too displeased with his 74.

Jose Maria Olazabal also had reason to be distracted early in his round when, together with Gil Morgan and Nick Price, they were confronted by a female streaker. Price got over it well enough to have a 69 but Morgan (72) and Olazabal (74) had less joy. The young lady got her picture in at least one newspaper, which seems to have been the main idea, and more column inches therefore than Ian Baker-Finch, whose 71 went largely unnoticed.

Rocco Mediate (above), impressive this year on the American tour, struggled for his 76. Mark Calcavecchia (below left) employed his wife Cheryl as his caddie, while twin brother Allan (below right) carried Curtis Strange's bag.

(Opposite page) Nick Price (top left) was challenging again in the Open Championship with his 69, while David Feherty (top right) was disappointed with his 79. Australians Mike Harwood (bottom left) and Wayne Grady were near the top with 68 and 69, respectively.

Wilson

PENTAX

Jamie Spence went out in 30 with four birdies, but finished with a 70, including a seven on the last hole.

FIRST ROUND RESULTS

HOLE	1	2	3	4	5	6	7	8	9	10	11	12	13	14	15	16	17	18	
PAR	4	4	4	3	4	4	3	4	4	4	4	3	4	3	5	4	5	4	TOTAL
Seve Ballesteros	4	4	4	3	3	4	3	4	4	3	4	3	5	2	6	4	3	3	66
Martin Gates	3	4	4	2	4	4	3	4	5	4	4	3	5	2	5	3	4	4	67
Chip Beck	4	5	4	4	3	4	3	3	3	4	3	3	4	3	4	5	4	4	67
Santiago Luna	5	4	3	3	3	4	4	3	4	4	4	3	3	3	6	3	3	5	67
Gary Hallberg	3	5	3	2	4	4	3	4	4	3	4	3	4	4	5	5	4	4	68
Mike Reid	4	4	4	3	4	5	3	4	4	4	3	4	4	3	4	4	4	3	68
Barry Lane	4	4	3	2	4	4	2	4	4	3	3	3	5	4	5	6	4	4	68
Nick Faldo	5	3	4	3	4	5	3	4	4	4	4	3	4	2	5	3	4	4	68
Costantino Rocca	4	4	3	3	4	4	3	4	4	4	4	3	4	3	5	4	4	4	68
Mark Mouland	5	3	3	4	5	4	2	4	4	4	4	3	3	3	6	4	4	3	68
Mike Harwood	4	3	4	2	4	5	3	3	4	3	4	3	4	3	5	4	5	5	68

HOLE SUMMARY

HOLE	PAR	EAGLES	BIRDIES	PARS	BOGEYS	HIGHER	RANK	AVERAGE
1	4	0	15	92	46	3	7	4.24
2	4	0	13	81	57	5	3	4.36
3	4	0	26	116	13	1	17	3.93
4	3	0	29	96	30	1	16	3.02
5	4	0	23	107	25	1	15	4.03
6	4	0	1	55	87	13	1	4.74
7	3	0	20	101	34	1	13	3.10
8	4	0	20	109	27	0	14	4.04
9	4	0	14	96	41	5	7	4.24
OUT	34	0	161	853	360	30		35.70
10	4	0	16	102	32	6	10	4.19
11	4	0	14	99	38	5	9	4.23
12	3	1	15	86	50	4	3	3.27
13	4	0	14	104	34	4	11	4.18
14	3	0	12	105	36	3	6	3.20
15	5	0	20	93	40	3	12	5.17
16	4	0	13	78	50	15	2	4.46
17	5	12	108	33	3	0	18	4.17
18	4	0	11	94	42	9	5	4.32
IN	36	13	223	794	325	49		37.19
TOTAL	70	13	384	1647	685	79		72.89

Players Below Par	17
Players At Par	11
Players Above Par	128

LOW SCORES

Low First Nine	Jamie Spence	30
Low Second Nine	Seve Ballesteros	33
	Nick Faldo	33
	Mike Reid	33
Low Round	Seve Ballesteros	66

Unexpected leaders included Costantino Rocca (left), Santiago Luna (right) and Martin Gates (opposite page).

FIRST-DAY WONDERS

BY MARINO PARASCENZO

Call him Santiago Who?

Actually, he's Santiago Luna, former unknown, now a bit better known. We were introduced to him in the first round of the Open Championship.

Someone said a Spaniard was tied for the lead. You were thinking Seve or Jose Maria, they said, 'no, it's Santiago Luna.' And you said, 'Santiago Who?'

Luna played his way on to the leaderboard with a 67, afterwards you couldn't tell him from a semi-nervous wreck. He looked like a greenhorn who had just peeled back his cards to find a full house.

There is a Santiago Luna in every major championship, and sometimes, a handful of them. They are no-names, or dimly obscure, at best. They are known but to family, friends and creditors. These are the First-Day Wonders. They surface magnificently, then disappear in a puff of nerves. If anything is a sure bet in golf, it is that at least one First-Day Wonder will explode on the scene, and then explode right back off it. There was no lack of them at Royal Birkdale.

Life on the leaderboard is an 'iffy' thing. To begin with, the thrill of seeing your name up there must be enough to drive a first-timer goofy (for the Open, multiply the effect by ten). You have to know how to handle it. The big boys do. It is just another day at the office. Tom Watson permits himself a hint of a self-satisfied smile. Nick Faldo and Raymond Floyd become almost friendly. Seve Ballesteros talks about being lucky. And so forth. It takes experience.

Luna, aged twenty-eight, hadn't been there. Neither had England's Martin Gates, a baby-faced rookie on the PGA European Tour and about a week from his twenty-seventh birthday. This was their first Open Championship. Just getting in was an accomplishment. They had to qualify. That's combat.

'If I had to play those qualifying rounds for a living,' Gates said, 'I wouldn't do it.'

Luna had just finished his round, and was meeting the Press corps for the first time, late in the afternoon. Ballesteros was still on the course at three under par.

'You're tied with Seve,' someone noted.

Luna – excitable, nervous – lit up. He rummaged around in his limited English, searching for a suitable acknowledgement. He couldn't find one, so he settled for a nod, a big grin, and '*Muy bien.*'

If he hadn't three-putted the eighteenth hole, it

(Previous page) Martin Gates set the early pace with a 67.

would have been a '*Muy-muy-muy bien*.' Without that bogey, he would have had a 66. He would have tied Ballesteros for the first-round lead.

Gates was in the second group off, at 7.25 a.m., and he was finished before Luna had even teed off five hours later. Gates wasn't merely the leader-in-the-clubhouse with that 67, he was the leader for about half the day.

'I didn't realize I was leading,' Gates said. 'I never looked at a scoreboard.'

The Press was watching him, though, and almost to a man, the question was – Who is Martin Gates?

The First-Day Wonders have to feel whipsawed. First, the whole world is watching. You are in the spotlight for the first time. That is a terribly naked feeling. And the heat from the Open Championship spotlight would make most strong men squirm. Second, there is a suspicion gnawing at you that you don't belong there. Sure, that's what you came for. Sure, you want to win. But this is the *Open*. You feel like a child sneaking on for a quick nine holes.

There are exceptions, of course. Look up Ballesteros, Severiano; 1976 Open, Royal Birkdale.

It seemed for a while that Luna and Gates would have to spend the night contemplating the sweet agony of leading the Open. They were at three-under-par 67, tied with an American, Chip Beck. Also up there were another pair known chiefly to family and close friends – Italy's Costantino Rocca (68) and the Scandinavian-sounding Brit, Carl Suneson (69).

Ballesteros saved them all. He came in late in the afternoon with a 66, and took the solo lead. That drew a lot of the heat off the First-Day Wonders. It also helped that defending champion Nick Faldo (68), Tom Watson (69), Wayne Grady (69) and Ian Woosnam (70) were up there.

Luna stole the show. He is as unknown as Ballesteros was in 1976. He is one of seven children, the son of an electrician at Puerta de Herro golf club in Madrid. He had little to show for his patchy days on the PGA European Tour. He had tried for his player's card five times, won it in 1984, lost it, won it back in 1990. And now he was having his finest year. In seventeen events, he had a career-best seventh place in the Madrid Open, plus three other top-ten finishes. He had missed the thirty-six hole cut eight times.

He was not a complete stranger to victory as a professional, if you count a minor Spanish championship, which he had won twice.

'He's a great golfer,' Ballesteros said.

Luna is certainly a determined one. He got into the Open like a gate crasher, and he made a little history in the bargain. He was part of the longest qualifying play-off in Open history. He shot 74,74 and was one of ten players on 148, fighting for the last three spots at Hillside. Luna won his place on the eighth extra hole. Then darkness fell, and the play-off dragged on into the next day. Spain's Yago Beamonte took the last spot over James Heggarty with a birdie on the sixteenth extra hole.

The world wasn't the only thing Luna surprised in the first round. He surprised himself, too. He tried to blot it all out.

Luna was going over his shots, hole-by-hole. The process seemed alien to him. He got through the first hole, but drew a blank on the second. He couldn't remember how he had played it.

'I come back to that,' he said, and he plunged on.

At the eighth hole, he drew another blank.

'That,' Burdman cracked, 'is why he made a low score.'

If Luna's 67 was a work of art, it was out of Dali – a surrealistic piece made up of four bogeys, five birdies and an eagle-three at the seventeenth. A strong tailwind had reduced the 525-yard hole practically to a drive and a pitch. Everyone was making birdies. A par was a dropped shot. Luna fired an eight iron in. 'How long was your putt?' he was asked.

He had been giving the length of his putts, but this time he merely spread his right hand, put it down on the table, then did it again.

'Like that,' he said. About eighteen inches.

Then came the eighteenth hole, and if he didn't already know he was leading the Open, he found out in a hurry. He marched into that historic setting – the cheering spectators in the grandstands, the flags whipping high overhead. Maybe it got to him.

He three-putted from forty feet. The bogey cost him a share of the lead with Ballesteros. It left him tied with Martin Gates, who had blazed the trail for the First-Day Wonders.

Gates and Luna were about 180 degrees apart. Luna was an electrician's son; Gates a banker's son. Luna came up as a caddie in Madrid; Gates was educated in the American college system. He was probably better known on the plains of Oklahoma than among the sand dunes of Royal Birkdale. Gates had played golf at the University of Oklahoma. He spent five years there, and earned a Bachelor's degree in marketing. 'I thought it would be useful in learning how to sell yourself,' Gates said.

He had won his PGA European Tour card on his second try, in 1990, and his first season had been so-so. In sixteen events, he had missed the thirty-six-hole cut seven times, and had one top-ten finish, a tie for fourth place in the Italian Open in mid-May. He also tied for twelfth in the Madrid Open, and his worst finish was sixty-fifth in the Spanish Open.

'Apart from being thrilled,' said Gates, after his first round of the Open, 'it was a tough day. I tried to keep the ball in the fairway, get it on the green, get down in two putts, and go on.'

He had a good game plan, but he wasn't figuring on a hot putter. He didn't even need it at the first hole. He chipped in from thirty feet, a nice start to your first Open, a birdie.

He one-putted for his other four birdies, including a forty-footer at the sixteenth hole, and needed just twenty-seven putts overall. He was perfect in the crucial six-to-ten foot range, going five-for-five. Two were for birdies, two to save par, and one to salvage bogey.

He bogeyed just twice. At the ninth hole, he tried to chip over some television cables and didn't make it. 'I should have had somebody hold them up,' Gates said. 'You live and learn.' At the thirteenth hole, his problems started with a drive into the rough and ended with his worst putting of the day – two putts from five feet.

Costantino Rocca was having a dandy season, his best since joining the tour in 1983. In sixteen events, he had missed only two cuts, finished third in the Italian Open, and had four other top-ten finishes. Now, if he could have just borrowed a couple of putts from Gates.

Rocca's 68 was a round of distinction. It was the only bogey-free round the first day (and one of only three in the entire Open). He had two birdies – a twenty-five foot putt and a tap-in. Now bite your putter in half. Rocca missed one birdie from four feet, two from nine feet, two from ten feet, and one from thirteen feet.

Suneson – almost nothing was known of him, except that he was British and not Swedish, and that he failed to win his player's card in 1990 – also claimed a distinction in his 69. He was the only player to run off four consecutive birdies in the first round – the fourteenth, fifteenth, sixteenth and seventeenth holes – and he double-bogeyed the thirteenth and bogeyed the eighteenth.

It couldn't last, and it didn't. By way of epilogue, Rocca shot five-over-par 285 and tied for forty-fourth place; Gates 288, tied for seventy-third; Luna 289, tied for eightieth, and Suneson 292, tied for ninety-sixth.

So there wasn't a Ballesteros in the bunch. Remember that Spanish teenage terror in 1976, thrashing Royal Birkdale to within a few shots of winning the Open? There wasn't an Ian Baker-Finch, either, the hyphenated wonder who stumbled into Swilcan Burn at St Andrews in the final round in 1984. He didn't stumble this time.

So their moment had come and gone. It can never be the same. But whatever happens, they will always know the paralysing thrill of that first day in the Open.

'I will always have the memories,' Gates said. 'To think that for one of the four days, I was in the limelight.'

The unknown Spaniard had put it another way. 'Are you nervous?' someone had asked.

'No,' Santiago Luna said. 'I am dreaming.'

Australian Mike Harwood had not played well this year, but was joint leader on 138.

DAY

2

AN UNEXPECTED TRIO ON TOP

BY MICHAEL WILLIAMS

The hands on the clock above the big scoreboard overlooking Royal Birkdale's eighteenth green had already passed 8.30 p.m. Only a sprinkling of inexhaustible spectators were still there, getting every last drop they could out of the second day's play. The evening had become grey and cool, and Mike Harwood, of Australia, and Gary Hallberg, of the United States, were well into, or even through, dinner. Both had again matched one another shot-for-shot, each now with second rounds of 70 to follow those of 68 the previous day. For some hours they had stood alone together on 138, two under par for the thirty-six holes.

Harwood had completed his 70 long before Andrew Oldcorn, a former English Amateur champion who could pass as a Scotsman since he has lived most of his life in Scotland, had even started his round. Hallberg was well into his second nine holes.

But it was Oldcorn, thirty-one years of age, who rewrote all the headlines and changed the stories which had already been written when, in the next-to-last group of the day, he came home with a 67 for a three-way tie of the lead. Behind that round, one of the lowest of the day, lay a story not just of fine driving, good iron play and holed putts, but one of human courage in the face of adversity.

In the winter of 1989, Oldcorn went down with influenza. Surprisingly, he could not shake it off after a week or so, and it lingered. He still felt far from well when he went to the first European tournament of the season in Tenerife. One evening he went out to dinner, and was hardly able to stand before he was taken back to his hotel. Oldcorn inevitably missed the cut and went home. There he was diagnosed as having contracted myalgic encephalomyelitis, which is better known as 'ME' or 'Yuppie flu' for its tendency to strike those in their twenties and thirties. He was out of tournament golf for a year.

At his worst, Oldcorn severely doubted whether he would ever play competitive golf again. 'The mental side is the hardest part to contend with,' he recalled. 'I was never in hospital, because there is no actual drug treatment for it. Some never recover. It starts off as a viral disease and affects your nervous system, even your brain.

'You have a lot of muscle wastage and you can't do anything. Your whole system packs in. Worst is not being able to read a newspaper or watch television or walk more than fifty yards outside the house. I just did not have the energy.'

The European Tour was sympathetic. They allowed Oldcorn to keep his player's card, and in 1990 he came back, though still very far from recovered. He played twelve tournaments, even finishing

(Previous page) Gary Hallberg birdied the last two holes.

joint eighth in the Benson and Hedges International. But it was the eight events in which he missed the cut that more accurately told of the misery he was still fighting. This time he lost his player's card.

Nonetheless, there had been a physical improvement in 1991, and when Oldcorn was accepted for two tournaments, he at least lasted the four days, though prize money of £1,512 did not do much more than cover his expenses.

Then Oldcorn, having qualified for the Open with rounds of 70 and 77 at Hesketh, enjoyed what he will regard as one of his finest hours, and one which he hoped would give victims of ME encouragement. 'I want this to be a signal to other people who get the disease that it is not a bottomless pit,' he said. 'You can get out of it. I want to be an example that, if you fight, you really can win.'

Here then was Oldcorn's first victory, the reward was the knowledge that in the third round he would be playing with Severiano Ballesteros. The Spaniard had fallen back with a 73 but was still nicely placed, a stroke behind Harwood, Hallberg and Oldcorn and alongside five others: A young British player, David Gilford, who had likewise recorded a 67 to follow his 72; two Americans in Mike Reid (68,70) and Mark O'Meara (71,68), and two Australians in Wayne Grady (69,70) and Steve Elkington (71,68).

These were the only players under par after a day in which the playing conditions of the morning were more difficult than the afternoon. The wind and occasional rain slowly abated, and roughly the same players, therefore, got the thin edge as the starting times were reversed.

On level par, together with Vijay Singh, of Fiji, were six British players in Howard Clark, Mark James, Richard Boxall, Colin Montgomerie, Barry Lane and Roger Chapman, whose 66 equalled the low round of the day by Bob Tway, of America.

The big guns were strangely muffled. Jose Maria Olazabal, of Spain, stirred himself with a 67 for a total of 141, three strokes off the lead, catching among others, Tom Watson, who took 72. Greg Norman, of Australia, had a 68 and that put him on 142 together with, again among others, Ian Baker-Finch (71), Ian Woosnam (72) and Bernhard Langer (71).

Nick Faldo fell back with a 75, Curtis Strange also lost ground with a 73, both of them now among another group on 143. Payne Stewart continued to keep a low profile with his second 72. It was all a very tangled picture, so tangled indeed that a record 113 players qualified for the last two rounds.

The championship rules are that the leading seventy players and ties go through. In 1986, the Royal and Ancient introduced an additional clause whereby all those within ten strokes of the leader should qualify. This did away with the second cut that used to be made after fifty-four holes. The forty-three additional players who, therefore, survived on 148 and better, were a costly crew for the R&A. Two of them, Phil Mickelson, of the United States, and Jim Payne, from Sandilands in Lincolnshire, were amateurs, but there were still another forty-one professionals, each of whom was now guaranteed a minimum £3,000 prize money rather than just the £600 they would have received for playing the first two rounds. It meant finding an extra £98,400, which raised the prize money from £900,000 to £998,400 – within a touch of being the first million-pound Open.

All this was not resolved until Oldcorn, in gathering gloom, had finished. If he had made a three at the last, he would have had a 66, a total of 137 and that would have knocked out all those on 148, numbering as they did sixteen, and including amongst others Tom Weiskopf, Tom Kite, Craig Stadler and Sam Torrance. Nor was Oldcorn far from it, for at the eighteenth he had bunkered his second shot left of the green but came out so deftly that his ball grazed the hole and stopped only two feet away, though he admitted later that the putt felt 'more like twenty feet.'

Teeing off as late as ten minutes past four is hardly ideal, but Oldcorn had a feeling that if he could get past the first six holes unscathed, 'the rest would take care of itself.' So it proved, as par followed par, and then he got his big lift, a two at the short seventh.

Weariness caught up with him after a four at the short twelfth, but another two at the fourteenth revived him, and his three at the sixteenth, where he hit a four iron to eight feet, and then a two-putt birdie at the seventeenth, brought him into a share of the lead alongside Harwood and Hallberg.

Harwood, a tall and lean Australian, had made his mark in Europe in 1990 when he won both the Volvo PGA Championship and the Volvo Masters. His 70 was compiled when the weather was at its least hospitable, particularly for a tall player who tends to get blown around more. However, he had regained some confidence after some lessons from Denis Pugh, of Quietwaters, and played the sort of steady game for which he is well known; three bogeys, three birdies and the rest pars.

Hallberg had a game plan before he went out. He decided on the practice ground that it was blowing so hard that he would have to keep the ball as low as possible. It did not go particularly well, one over par for nine holes and then a double bogey five at the twelfth, with three putts. It changed his whole approach.

Thereafter Hallberg forgot all about the wind and keeping the ball low. He went back to his normal game, hitting it high and hoping for the best. His reward was not long in coming, with a four iron he aimed out over the grandstands at the fourteenth so that the wind brought it back to within eight feet of the flag, from where he holed for a two. Then he played a nicely judged running chip to the seventeenth for his four, and rounded it all off with a putt of thirty feet for a birdie at the eighteenth as well.

After that tremendous finish on Thursday, Ballesteros was quickly brought back to earth, dropping two strokes in his first two holes and then a third at the sixth. This was not at all according to plan. A birdie at the ninth perked him up, though he continued to have to fight to keep his head above water. Only a lovely little chip from the back of the green at the tenth saved his par, and it took a brave putt to do so again at the eleventh, where he overdid his attempt to cut a long iron and missed the green on the right.

This was nevertheless fighting stuff, and it continued at the fifteenth as a sudden squall lengthened the hole even further. As in the first round, Ballesteros again played 'safe' with an iron from the tee. Yet he still found one of the bunkers lurking on the left-hand side, came out well but then hooked again left of the green. Another brave putt saved his par and, as he strode to the sixteenth green, he happened to catch my eye, puffing out his cheeks as he did so with a quite audible 'phew'.

If this seemed to indicate that the crisis was passed, it was not. Off the sixteenth tee, which presented a real tiger of a shot over 200 yards of heavy rough, he came right off his drive and beat his thigh with disgust as his ball carved its way deep into the willow scrub not far from where in 1961 Arnold Palmer played such an heroic recovery that a plaque now marks the spot.

Ballesteros' ball was quite unplayable but fortunately there was an adjacent sandy path and after an interminable time, during which the spectators were finally shifted on to the fairway so that he could get a sight of the green, he played a great shot just short of the green and got away with a five. It could so easily have been anything.

Nevertheless it was another shot gone, and nor was it retrieved at the seventeenth. There he was at odds with his caddie over whether it was an eight or a seven iron to the green. He stuck to his choice of an eight but the seeds of doubt were there and, in trying to hit it too hard, he dragged the shot into a bunker. Ballesteros remained buoyant. 'My position is just where I want to be; the best possible,' he said.

Grady, having reached the turn in 33 despite a double-bogey six at the first hole, went two under par for the round with a three at the tenth. Thereafter he played what he called a 'load of rubbish' for the remaining six holes and was delighted to get away with a 70. Elkington, his fellow Australian, put on his spurt over the last four holes with a birdie at the fifteenth and an eagle-three at the seventeenth. He would have tied the lead, but missed a putt of no more than two feet at the last for what would have been a 67.

O'Meara, on the course where he had won the Lawrence Batley International tournament in 1987, was very much at home with a 68. Reid stayed well in the hunt as well with a 71, while Gilford joined it with a splendid 67. Gilford had avoided the trials of

(Opposite page) A former winner at Royal Birkdale, Mark O'Meara (top left), was also on 139, joining the group that included David Gilford (top right) and Seve Ballesteros (bottom), who was three over par for the second round.

Mike Reid (left) and Wayne Grady were both on 139, in the group one stroke off the lead.

TOYOTA

having to qualify with a high finish in the previous week's Bell's Scottish Open and this was the first time he had made it into the last two rounds.

Other than a drive into the rough at the sixth and a three iron wide of the eleventh green, Gilford played extremely well with six birdies altogether, three on either side. Only two however were the result of long putts, the rest all very much shorter, and one of them, at the fifth hole for a three, from only two inches.

Tway did even better than that. His 66 included an eagle-two at the eighth, where he sank a seven iron from 190 yards. Since he had just made a two as well at the seventh, that was only four hits of the ball in two holes – an economy of striking that is hard to better. Since he was playing in the group immediately behind Ballesteros, Tway faced equally difficult conditions and showed what could be done. It also made a welcome change, for the Open is not an event in which he had previously distinguished himself.

Chapman, one of Europe's 'nearly men', had a 66 as well, and that delighted him because after a first round of 74 he knew he was in danger of missing the cut. He certainly had his eye with his putter. He holed from off the green at the third for his first birdie, sank others of twenty feet at the seventh and eleventh, and a putt of fifteen feet for an eagle at the seventeenth. His only bad hole was the sixth, where he was bunkered from the tee.

Though British interest in the championship remained healthy, it was not coming from its anticipated quarter. Faldo claimed his putting had let him down as he tumbled backwards with a 75. Most of the damage was done in the first six holes, where he dropped four strokes. He also took a double bogey at the short twelfth, with three putts after first missing the green. Half the time Faldo could not read the line of his putts and, if he did, he couldn't stroke the ball as intended.

Woosnam had given the appearance of getting back into the picture when he went out in 33 but he was destroyed by the six he took at the thirteenth, shanking a seven iron into the scrub and having to take a penalty drop. 'It got to me,' he admitted. 'I'm not playing well at all . . . hitting the ball all over the place. But that's golf.'

An equally costly six came from Watson, who had got back the two shots he had dropped going out and was in line for a 70 when he came to the last hole. A par four there would have left him only a shot behind the leaders but, from the eighteenth tee, he cut a one iron and his golf ball was unplayable, close to the out-of-bounds fence. Nor was it the sort of place where he could find a much better lie with a penalty drop. He did not reach the green until his fourth shot and a potentially very challenging position was lost.

Nevertheless, Watson was still only three strokes behind, with altogether thirty-eight players within four strokes of the leaders. Among them, still attracting no particular attention, remained Ian Baker-Finch.

Mark James was on level-par 140 after his 68 in the second round.

Greg Norman (142)

Ian Baker-Finch (142)

Jose Maria Olazabal (141)

Fred Couples (141)

Nick Faldo (143)

Neither Raymond Floyd (left) nor Sandy Lyle survived the thirty-six-hole cut-off.

SECOND ROUND RESULTS

HOLE	1	2	3	4	5	6	7	8	9	10	11	12	13	14	15	16	17	18	
PAR	4	4	4	3	4	4	3	4	4	4	4	3	4	3	5	4	5	4	TOTAL
Mike Harwood	5	3	4	3	4	5	3	4	4	4	4	2	4	3	5	5	4	4	70-138
Gary Hallberg	4	4	4	3	4	4	3	4	5	4	4	5	4	2	5	4	4	3	70-138
Andrew Oldcorn	4	4	4	3	4	4	2	4	4	4	4	4	4	2	5	3	4	4	67-138
Seve Ballesteros	5	5	4	3	4	5	3	4	3	4	4	3	4	3	5	5	5	4	73-139
Mike Reid	5	4	4	3	4	4	4	4	4	4	4	3	4	3	4	5	4	4	71-139
David Gilford	4	4	3	3	3	5	2	4	5	4	5	2	4	3	4	4	4	4	67-139
Wayne Grady	6	3	4	2	4	4	2	4	4	3	5	4	5	3	5	4	4	4	70-139
Steve Elkington	5	4	4	2	4	5	3	4	4	4	4	3	4	3	4	4	3	4	68-139
Mark O'Meara	4	4	4	3	5	4	3	4	3	5	4	3	4	4	5	3	3	3	68-139

HOLE SUMMARY

HOLE	PAR	EAGLES	BIRDIES	PARS	BOGEYS	HIGHER	RANK	AVERAGE
1	4	0	6	74	68	8	2	4.51
2	4	0	12	73	58	13	4	4.46
3	4	1	20	119	16	0	17	3.96
4	3	0	10	121	24	1	13	3.10
5	4	0	22	94	33	7	10	4.17
6	4	0	4	64	69	19	1	4.67
7	3	0	21	98	33	4	9	3.13
8	4	1	13	121	19	2	15	4.05
9	4	0	22	107	19	8	14	4.10
OUT	**34**	**2**	**130**	**871**	**339**	**62**		**36.15**
10	4	0	14	91	48	3	8	4.26
11	4	0	12	95	43	6	7	4.28
12	3	0	13	99	38	6	5	3.24
13	4	0	14	108	28	6	10	4.17
14	3	0	16	108	29	3	12	3.12
15	5	0	25	103	25	3	16	5.04
16	4	0	8	77	62	9	3	4.48
17	5	11	102	41	2	0	18	4.22
18	4	0	11	98	37	9	6	4.30
IN	**36**	**11**	**215**	**820**	**312**	**45**		**37.11**
TOTAL	**70**	**13**	**345**	**1691**	**651**	**107**		**73.26**

Steve Elkington (left) came home in 33 for a 68, while Robert Gamez (right) went out in 32 but finished with a 72.

Players Below Par	19
Players At Par	8
Players Above Par	128

LOW SCORES

Low First Nine	Robert Gamez	32
	Mark James	32
	Greg Norman	32
	Bob Tway	32
Low Second Nine	Roger Chapman	33
	Darren Clarke	33
	Fred Couples	33
	Steve Elkington	33
	Jose Maria Olazabal	33
	Peter Senior	33
	Andrew Sherborne	33
Low Round	Roger Chapman	66
	Bob Tway	66

Playing in the Open was Andrew Oldcorn's goal for the year, and he gave hope to other victims of ME.

A VICTORY JUST TO BE HERE

BY ALISTER NICOL

When Andrew Oldcorn filed his entry for the Open Championship early in 1991, he had no inkling of the waves he would create at Royal Birkdale by tieing for the halfway lead with a 67 late in the evening. That three-under-par effort saw him join Australian Mike Harwood and American Gary Hallberg, who both shot 70, at the top of the scoreboard.

It also invoked the Royal and Ancient's ten-shot rule for the first time since the rule was introduced in 1986. The rule says that all players within ten shots of the lead qualify for the two final rounds. So, a record 113 players contested the final thirty-six holes, courtesy of Andy Oldcorn.

The fact that his recovery from a greenside bunker at the eighteenth hole spun from the lip of the cup instead of dropping for a birdie-three and a championship-leading 66 was but a minor irritation for the thirty-one-year-old English-born, Edinburgh-based Oldcorn, because even as he filled in his entry form, he was unsure whether he would even be able to compete in the qualifying rounds. 'Just to be here is a major achievement,' he said that Friday evening.

The winter of 1990–91 was a bad one for Oldcorn. Indeed, he had lived through a nightmare for thirty harrowing months, frequently worrying whether he would ever again compete at golf's highest level, for in February, 1989, he had contracted the mysterious and enfeebling post-viral fatigue syndrome.

The medical term is myalgic encephalomyelitis, abbreviated to ME. It has the medical profession totally baffled. Some doctors refuse to accept it as a genuine illness, even though sufferers such as Oldcorn know from bitter and anxious experience that it is a seriously debilitating disease. Many medical men are sceptical of ME, some downright dismissive.

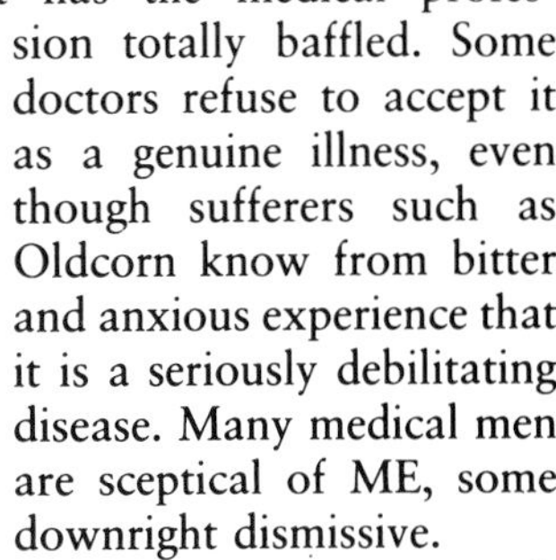

'Believe me, it is real, whatever it is, whatever causes the illness,' Oldcorn said. 'It all started when I picked up a virus during the Tenerife Open in the Canary Islands in February, 1989. I began to feel totally listless, completely drained of energy. I kept trying to play, but it was impossible I simply ran out of steam after only a few holes. I did not have the energy to go to the practice range at Dalmahoy, only a few miles from my Edinburgh home. I did not have a clue what was happening to me, and neither did my local doctor.

'Things became so bad that at times I did not have the concentration to read a newspaper all the way through or even watch a television programme to the end. Walking fifty yards exhausted me completely so golf, especially tournament play, was completely out of the question. I was nearly out of my mind with

(Previous page) Despite setbacks, Oldcorn was pleased.

worry on occasions. But deep down I don't think I ever gave up hope.'

Determined not to surrender to his illness, Oldcorn doggedly entered the Benson and Hedges International at York in May, 1989, and shot a third-round 66 to finish joint sixteenth – his best tournament of an agonizing year. That performance took a heavy toll, however, and following it he approached PGA European Tour officials.

Fortunately, the Tour, of which he has been a member since 1983, when he won the qualifying tournament after a brilliant amateur career, proved a caring, kind and considerate body.

After his 1991 Open Championship exploits, Oldcorn explained, 'I put my case at length to Executive Director Ken Schofield, and the Tournament Committee agreed that I should go home, rest up, get well again and forget all about playing sufficient tournaments and winning enough money to retain my playing privileges on the Tour. In effect, they granted me a year's dispensation.'

That sabbatical lifted a huge burden from his shoulders, but unfortunately did nothing to improve his worsening medical condition. As yet there is no known antidote to ME.

A growing number of researchers are beginning to believe that most sufferers have indeed been affected by a virus – perhaps such as the one Oldcorn picked up in Tenerife in early 1989 – which may persist long after the initial infection. It can, it is now believed, attack the muscles and affect the brain as well.

'Depression is definitely a major side effect. In fact I can put my finger precisely on the time I began my slow recovery, which is by no means complete,' Oldcorn said after the Open. 'It was the day in 1990 when my local GP suggested I try a course of anti-depressant drugs. That infuriated me. I vowed to myself I would never resort to any kind of drugs, I would beat the illness myself if humanly possible.'

One result of his showing in the 1989 Benson and Hedges was an invitation to the 1990 tournament, held that year at St Mellion in Cornwall. The layout, mainly on the floor of a deep valley, is arguably the most difficult walking course on the entire PGA European Tour. Despite his illness, Oldcorn shot a record-equalling 65 in the second round and finished tied for eighth.

'I was very pleased with that performance, because it proved that I could still play well, but I suffered agonies that week,' Oldcorn said. 'My legs kept cramping up and after each day's play I simply collapsed in bed and slept for at least twelve hours. I knew I was nowhere near full recovery.'

There was to be an unusual and unexpected spin-off, however. His 65 drew media attention and the ME was given wide exposure in the sporting Press. That in turn led to a fellow-sufferer in York writing to Oldcorn, offering sympathy and encouragement. She also suggested he undergo a specific blood test.

'At that time there was only one laboratory in the country conducting the test and, although my doctor did not want me to do it, I sent a blood sample privately. It cost me £80, but it was money well spent because the test showed I had violent reactions to certain foods,' Oldcorn said. 'They were mainly dairy products, but also tea and coffee and, of all things, salmon. So I altered my diet quite drastically and a slow improvement began, helped by advice and encouragement from an Edinburgh doctor, Alistair Fraser, who specializes in viral complaints.'

Oldcorn, once affectionately known as 'Beachball' because of his girth and bouncy good humour, lost around three stone as a result of his weakening illness, but rest, his change of diet and continual comfort from family and friends gradually saw him regain his strength.

Last autumn, he still did not feel up to returning to the qualifying tournament to try for his player's card. Indeed, six months before the Open Championship, he struggled to play a friendly nine holes at Dalmahoy, the course where as a teenager he once beat former Walker Cup star Scott McDonald in the first round of the club championship.

Although he left Lancashire as a nine year old when his family moved to the village of Balerno, on the outskirts of Edinburgh, and regards himself nowadays as a Scot, Oldcorn clearly retains an affinity for the country of his birth. He played Boys and Youth golf for England, won the first Scottish Open

Amateur Stroke Play in 1979, then won the English Amateur Championship at Hoylake in 1982. That success earned him a place in the England side and the 1983 Walker Cup.

He turned pro later in 1983 and, as recorded above, won the Tour's qualifying tournament that autumn. Steady if unspectacular progress followed, and in 1987 came his best Tour performance, at Royal Birkdale.

'I shot 68, 68, 71, 68 to finish thirteen under par and third, four shots behind Mark O'Meara, who twice holed full seven-iron shots for eagles in his last-round 66,' Oldcorn said. 'I fell in love with Birkdale that week and I think it will always be my favourite course, because it is so tough but fair. That's one reason I was anxious to do well in this year's Open.'

He survived the qualifying test by one stroke at Hesketh then, astonishingly, changed his irons before the Open. The switch did no harm, as he shot an opening 71. 'And I was confident going into the second round. My young brother Alistar, himself a two-handicapper, was my caddie and we worked well as a team,' Oldcorn said. 'My plan was to get through the first six holes in par, if possible, and I felt good when I struck my opening tee shot with a five wood into the ideal spot in the fairway.'

The game plan worked perfectly, and he holed a twenty-foot birdie putt at the short seventh. A further two at the fourteenth balanced out a dropped shot at the twelfth and, although tiring, made a superb three at the difficult par-four sixteenth. 'I knew the long seventeenth was on for another birdie as it was playing directly downwind, and I just missed an eagle in fact from ten feet,' he said. 'I made the six-inch return though for my third birdie in four holes in tough conditions.'

One more birdie and Oldcorn would have taken the outright lead. He pulled both his drive and then his approach shot into a bunker left of the green. He had been in the same bunker four years previously, when he finished third behind O'Meara, and taken five. 'This time it was a much easier shot, and I honestly thought I had holed it,' he said.

The fact that he made four kept thirteen other players in the championship, including Sweden's Magnus Persson and Scots Stephen McAllister and Sam Torrance. The next morning, all three sought him out to give thanks for guaranteeing them at least £3,000, and Torrance told him, 'Well done last night. I know you are playing with Seve Ballesteros today and that will be difficult. But just go out there, play your own game and enjoy yourself.'

Oldcorn shot 77 in the presence of Ballesteros and his noisy gallery, and did not enjoy the experience one iota. However, he thoroughly relished his Friday 67 and his moments of glory. They gave him renewed hope that his long struggle against ME was nearing an end, and that despite the mystery illness robbing him of two years at a vital time in his career there was, at last, brightness glowing at the end of a very long, very dark and despairing tunnel.

He said, 'I still tire quickly and easily, but I have proven I can compete again with the best and, most importantly of all, I have shown that ME can be beaten.'

An eagle-birdie finish enabled Mark O'Meara to share the third-round lead with Ian Baker-Finch.

DAY

3

FRIENDS, NEIGHBOURS AND LEADERS

BY MICHAEL WILLIAMS

After two rounds of the 1984 Open Championship at St Andrews, the field was led by such a little-known Australian that one British tabloid newspaper, in an attempt to be clever, put up the back-page headline: 'Ian Baker-Who?' Its golf correspondent was apparently not much the wiser either, for the first paragraph of his story then read: 'Ian Baker-Smith yesterday led the Open with rounds of 68 and 66.'

Thus did Ian Baker-Finch first arrive on the golfing scene, his anonymity at that time tending to be confirmed when, after he had held on with a third round of 71 for a share of the lead with Tom Watson, he subsided to a last round of 79. It relegated him to equal ninth place, as Severiano Ballesteros took the second of his three titles by two strokes from Watson and Bernhard Langer.

Baker-Finch, a tall man of striking good looks, had to live with that memory for a number of years, though he must always have wondered what a different story it might have been but for the piece of bad luck he had suffered, when, partnered by Watson in the last group, he played his second shot to the first green. It was finely judged, just over the Swilcan Burn, but such was the spin he had on the ball that it spun back into the water.

This was not the only time one of golf's true gentlemen had the experience of going out last on the final day. In 1990, again at St Andrews, Baker-Finch partnered Nick Faldo, though in this instance his prospects were not as promising. Faldo already had a lead of five strokes and won by five, though not from Baker-Finch whose 76 dropped him back this time into a share of sixth place.

Now at Royal Birkdale, opportunity beckoned a third time for Baker-Finch as, with a third round of 64, he emerged from the pack to share the lead with Mark O'Meara, whose 67 gave him the same total, 206, four under par, for the fifty-four holes.

If the Open Championship had for two days taken no particular shape, it had at last come to life as, on a day that at last had a touch of summer about it, no less than thirty players scored in the 60s as the sprint for the finishing tape began in earnest.

It was, for all that, not quite the leaderboard that had been expected before the Championship began. That gentle, ambling Irishman, Eamonn Darcy, was leading the home challenge after a 66 that took him to within a stroke of the two leaders, together with a second Australian, Mike Harwood, who had 69. More significant, it seemed at the time, was the continuing presence of Ballesteros, whose 69 kept him nicely tucked in two strokes behind.

(Previous page) HRH the Duke of York and Michael Bonallack.

Next, on 209, came Vijay Singh, of Fiji, together with a second American in Mike Reid, while of the four players on 210, level par, three of them were British in Martin Poxon (67), Mark Mouland (68) and Mark James (70). The quartet was made up by Craig Parry (69), a third Australian and winner of the previous week's tournament, the Bell's Scottish Open at Gleneagles. Looking down this list, one American observer remarked, 'I see we have only one more player in the top ten than Fiji!'

The day was marred by a most unusual accident. Richard Boxall, whose opening rounds of 71 and 69 had given him a lively interest in the Championship, was only three strokes off the lead when he stepped on the ninth tee. He then drove perfectly down the middle, but there was then a second crack as he completed his swing and he collapsed on the ground with what turned out to be a broken left leg.

According to his caddie, Andy Bladen, Boxall had felt some discomfort in the leg before going out to play and it worsened after he had driven at the sixth. This was confirmed by Andrew Chandler, Boxall's manager, who said, 'Richard said he felt all right but his left leg was bothering him.' The injury put Boxall, who was eighty-eighth on the European money list and in need therefore of a substantial cheque, out of action for the year.

Since the field was now playing in twos, it meant that Colin Montgomerie no longer had a partner and he played on for two holes by himself, accompanied by a Rules official, John Uzielli, a past winner of the Oxford and Cambridge Golfing Society's President's Putter. The R&A had five options.

The first was that Montgomerie continue to play alone (his card being marked by the Rules official); the second that Mr Uzielli's clubs be fetched so that he could play; a third that a marker be sent out to accompany him; a fourth that he drop back to make up a threeball with Mark James and Roger Chapman; and, a fifth that he move up to join Barry Lane and Vijay Singh.

Montgomerie's preference was to join other competitors, and as James and Chapman were not, apparently, enthusiastic, he therefore played 'catch-up golf' for two holes before joining Lane and Singh. It was not something he particularly enjoyed, and even less so when he dropped a shot at the tenth. The delay may also have disturbed Lane's rhythm for, when Montgomerie joined up, Lane promptly dropped two strokes at the eleventh. Both were challenging the leaders at the time and each finished in 71.

Baker-Finch came from four strokes behind the two overnight leaders, Harwood and Gary Hallberg, and played an hour and forty-five minutes before them. 'I really did not think the course was very difficult today,' he said afterwards. 'The conditions were very similar to what they had been in practice and I'm surprised not to see Seve, Bernhard (Langer), Greg (Norman) or Nick (Faldo) make a real charge.'

Baker-Finch was into his stride immediately. He had birdies at the second, third and fifth holes, twice holing putts of twenty feet, and at the third one of six feet as he pitched over the guardian bunker with a nine-iron second shot. Three putts at the short seventh was an interruption, but Pete Bender, who caddied for Norman when he won at Turnberry in 1986, urged his man to be patient, pointing out that a lot of people were going to miss short putts on greens that were causing problems, particularly at short range.

Sure enough, Baker-Finch three-putted once again at the fourteenth, but by then he had made two more birdies. He had hit a glorious five iron to eight feet at the tenth, a seven iron to two feet at the thirteenth and then went into overdrive for the last two holes, each time his five iron was the ace club in his bag. It enabled him to reach the seventeenth green in two before he holed from twenty feet for an eagle, while at the last he was even closer, this time five feet from where he sank the putt for a birdie.

'Being in the final pair again is another goal achieved,' he said afterwards. 'In 1984 I was just a starry-eyed kid having a great time. Last year I was a little bit bigger kid and learned a hell of a lot from the guy who won (Faldo). I have improved even more since then, and have a lot to thank Nick for. Just watching him go on and win and the way he went about was an education.

'I learned I needed to be a bit more focused on what I was doing and not to allow outside influences to upset me. I knew that before, but sometimes you need a kick in the pants to jog the memory. Nick was focused on his job and I was just a marker by his side. I remember the procession of carts, the dust, and it bothered me. It didn't worry Nick. He just concentrated on his work and got on with it.'

It was a happy coincidence that O'Meara should share the lead with Baker-Finch, for they are close friends and also neighbours in Florida. O'Meara's other delight was that he was even playing. The previous weekend he had been in two minds about making the flight to England at all.

For some time he had been suffering from an inflamed cartilage in his rib cage, and had hardly played any competitive golf since the US Open the previous month. Physiotherapy helped, but on the morning he was due to leave his Orlando home, he was in such pain that he was on the point of cancelling. Two things made up his mind; he liked Birkdale because he had won a tournament there in 1987, and he did not want to disappoint his daughter, who had never been to England.

On the eve of the Championship, O'Meara limited himself to hitting just a few balls on the practice ground. Even after his first round of 71, he still had half a mind to scratch, such was his discomfort when he came off the golf course. The uncertainty persisted even as he walked to the tee for his second round; but then he had a 68, and he hardly felt a thing, any more than he did in his third round of 67. Beware the injured has long been a golfing doctrine.

Even so, it took O'Meara a little time to get going, with dropped shots at the second and sixth. He made twos at the seventh and fourteenth, and then joined the handicap brigade. From an admittedly rather bare lie short and left of the sixteenth green, his little chip was horribly fluffed and he had to chip again to escape with a bogey five. However, all this was quickly put at the back of his mind as, like Baker-Finch, he finished eagle-birdie for his 67 and a share of the lead.

Darcy was tickled to death at being so closely involved. In his previous sixteen Opens, his best finish had been equal eleventh in 1985, when Sandy Lyle won at Royal St George's. His swing is as Irish as they come – 'all my own work,' he says with a grin – and with his feet angled at 'ten to two' he ambles round the course in as relaxed a manner as he does on his country walks with his two beloved red setters.

Here is another sufferer of a back condition. Darcy had to withdraw from the Carrolls Irish Open after only one round. Now, however, he was off to a real flier with birdies at the first, fifth, sixth and eighth holes, which gave him a good chance of being out in 30. His approach putt at the ninth came up short, and he missed the next putt from perhaps five feet.

Darcy exchanged a birdie with a bogey at the twelfth and thirteenth, but he cut loose with two drives up the fifteenth, chipped up close for his four and looked very much on for a 65. He found a bad place in a bunker at the seventeenth, and had to settle for the par that on this hole always feels like a dropped shot.

Ballesteros again had an indifferent start with shots dropped at both the fourth and fifth holes. He was in grand form after that, inching his way back with birdies at the eighth and twelfth, where he hit a gorgeous five iron to a yard, and made sure he broke 70 again with a four at the seventeenth.

Two strokes behind the leaders, Ballesteros saw this as a great position from which to mount his assault the following day. 'I don't think I have to attack from here,' he remarked. He sensed the crowd was on his side, which they undoubtedly were, and his sixth sense was that all he had to do was wait for those in front to come back to him. 'They may not be afraid of me,' Ballesteros said, 'but they may be of the trophy.' It all sounded plausible enough, even if one did have an uneasy feeling that fate might now have been tempted.

Harwood has no illusions about being one of the great players, but he continued to hang on for his 69 and he alone had not yet exceeded par in any of his three rounds. Not that those prospects were exactly rosy when he went to three over par after consecutive

Ian Baker-Finch tees off in his round of 64, which included six birdies, one eagle and two bogeys.

dropped shots at the eleventh and twelfth holes.

It is amazing, however, what a banana or two will do. As Harwood trudged to the thirteenth tee, his spirits low, his wife mentioned to him that he had not eaten anything. So he dived into his bag, scoffed a couple of bananas and away he went, birdie, birdie, par, birdie, birdie, par, and there he was right back in the picture again.

While Singh, with a 69, and an American, Mike Reid (70), were continuing to keep in touch, there was still no move from the more fancied runners, though Ian Woosnam kept some faint hopes alive with a 69, before he muttered dark things about the greens, which is to be expected of someone who did not hole too many putts. Nor did Faldo, who twice three-putted from twenty feet in his 70, that being the outer extremity of his birdie zone. 'Ridiculous,' he lamented.

Payne Stewart was another who still could not get the hang of things, even if he did make a one-stroke improvement on his first two rounds of 72.

Jack Nicklaus, as always, never gave an inch, and got under par for the first time with a 69. It meant that on the last day Nicklaus was drawn to

Mike Harwood (top right) was driving straight, if not long, while taking a share of third place with his 69.

Richard Boxall was just two strokes off the lead when he fractured his left leg while driving off the ninth tee.

Vijay Singh (bottom right) gave Fiji a man in the top ten with his 69 for fifth place, two shots behind the leaders.

play with Jim Payne, the British Youths champion. Payne did not really believe it when he rang the club to find out his tee time, for he had other things on his mind. His third round of 70 had given him an unexpected three-stroke lead over the American amateur, Phil Mickelson, and the silver medal was now a realistic dream. But to win it in the company of Nicklaus. Now that would be something.

Seve Ballesteros felt he was well-placed after his 69 for fifth place, two strokes behind the leaders.

Frustrated on the greens, Greg Norman returned a 71.

Tied at level-par 210 were (clockwise from bottom left): Mark James, Craig Parry and Martin Poxon. Isao Aoki (below) did not play in the Open Championship, but was a commentator for Japanese television.

Mark Mouland was on a roller-coaster in his round of 68, after going three over par on the first two holes.

THIRD ROUND RESULTS

HOLE	1	2	3	4	5	6	7	8	9	10	11	12	13	14	15	16	17	18	
PAR	**4**	**4**	**4**	**3**	**4**	**4**	**3**	**4**	**4**	**4**	**4**	**3**	**4**	**3**	**5**	**4**	**5**	**4**	**TOTAL**
Ian Baker-Finch	4	3	3	3	3	4	4	4	4	3	4	3	3	4	5	4	3	3	**64-206**
Mark O'Meara	4	5	4	3	4	5	2	4	4	4	4	2	4	3	4	5	3	3	**67-206**
Eamonn Darcy	3	4	4	3	3	3	3	3	5	4	4	2	5	3	4	4	5	4	**66-207**
Mike Harwood	4	5	4	3	4	3	3	4	5	4	5	4	3	2	5	3	4	4	**69-207**
Seve Ballesteros	4	4	4	4	5	4	3	3	4	4	4	2	4	3	5	4	4	4	**69-208**
Vijay Singh	4	3	4	3	5	4	3	4	4	4	4	3	3	3	5	4	5	4	**69-209**
Mike Reid	5	4	4	4	4	5	3	4	4	4	4	2	4	2	4	4	5	4	**70-209**
Martin Poxon	5	4	5	2	3	5	2	4	4	4	4	3	4	2	5	4	3	4	**67-210**
Mark Mouland	6	5	3	4	3	4	3	3	3	3	4	3	4	2	4	4	5	5	**68-210**
Craig Parry	5	4	4	2	4	4	3	4	4	4	4	3	4	3	4	5	4	4	**69-210**
Mark James	4	4	4	3	4	4	3	5	4	4	6	3	4	3	4	4	4	3	**70-210**

HOLE SUMMARY

HOLE	PAR	EAGLES	BIRDIES	PARS	BOGEYS	HIGHER	RANK	AVERAGE
1	4	0	9	60	38	6	2	4.36
2	4	0	11	76	23	3	8	4.16
3	4	0	23	83	7	0	16	3.86
4	3	0	8	76	26	3	3	3.21
5	4	0	16	79	18	0	12	4.02
6	4	0	7	49	52	5	1	4.51
7	3	0	25	76	11	1	17	2.89
8	4	0	12	77	22	2	9	4.12
9	4	0	19	66	24	3	10	4.10
OUT	**34**	**0**	**130**	**642**	**221**	**23**		**35.23**
10	4	0	14	87	10	1	13	4.00
11	4	0	17	64	23	8	6	4.20
12	3	0	16	73	23	0	11	3.06
13	4	0	24	65	22	1	13	4.00
14	3	0	9	78	24	1	6	3.15
15	5	1	31	64	14	2	15	4.88
16	4	0	10	70	29	3	4	4.22
17	5	9	71	30	2	0	18	4.22
18	4	0	12	67	31	2	5	4.21
IN	**36**	**10**	**204**	**598**	**178**	**18**		**35.94**
TOTAL	**70**	**10**	**334**	**1240**	**399**	**41**		**71.17**

Davis Love III went out in 30, then took an eight on the par-four tenth hole.

Paul Broadhurst shot 32 on the second nine for his 68.

Players Below Par	30
Players At Par	17
Players Above Par	65

LOW SCORES

Low First Nine	Davis Love III	30
Low Second Nine	Ian Baker-Finch	32
	Paul Broadhurst	32
	Mark O'Meara	32
	Brett Ogle	32
	Jamie Spence	32
Low Round	Ian Baker-Finch	64

The leading European in the Open, Eamonn Darcy tied for fifth place, including a 66 in the third round.

EUROPE'S UNLIKELY LEADER

BY RENTON LAIDLAW

The chance of a player doing well in any event is improved if he feels comfortable on the course, and thirty-nine-year-old Eamonn Darcy, who ended up as the top European in the 1991 Open Championship, felt at ease with Royal Birkdale from the moment he arrived at the Lancashire venue.

Royal Birkdale is not his favourite course. Royal St George's, on the south coast of England, where he chased Arnold Palmer home in the 1975 PGA Championship and lost a play-off to Neil Coles in the same event a year later, is the Open venue he likes best.

Significantly, until 1991, his eleventh place in the 1985 Open, won by Sandy Lyle at Sandwich, had been his best performance in the Championship, but Royal Birkdale had always come a close second in his opinion to Royal St George's.

Why does a golfer feel more at home on one course than another? Darcy, who turned pro in 1969, cannot explain, but he does know why he liked it this time. He had less fear of the tricky four-footers on the surprisingly spongy greens than most others in the field.

It did turn out to be a week, as Tom Kite said, when the good putters two-putted and the bad ones did too, levelling everyone out for a time – a fact the R&A appreciated when 113 players made the halfway cut.

Where Darcy had an advantage over most of his rivals was that allied to his confident work on the greens, he played exceptionally solidly to them. He did not make many mistakes. In addition, he enjoyed himself – more than he ever expected to. Four weeks earlier, there seemed every chance he would not be able to play at all.

Finishing as the top European never crossed his mind. All he thought of that week at Southport was winning the title that had always eluded Irishman Harry Bradshaw, beaten by Bobby Locke in a play-off in 1949. He was, from the moment he teed off on the first day, interested only in getting Alex Harvey to engrave his name on the famous claret jug. Not too many Pressmen, except those from Ireland whose support the golfers from the country enjoy so much, gave Eamonn much pre-Championship space.

All the European talk was of Nick Faldo, the defending champion, Masters champion Ian Woosnam and the Spaniards, Jose Maria Olazabal, even though he had indicated he was not playing well, and more significantly, the back-to-form Seve Ballesteros. They were the European favourites.

Darcy was a long shot to win, and it was felt he might not even make the halfway cut if still suffering

(Previous page) World No. 1 Ian Woosnam was nine strokes behind.

from a back problem. The complaint had somewhat embarrassingly forced him to withdraw from the Carroll's Irish Open at Killarney a month earlier and to miss the chance of playing in the French Open and at Monte Carlo.

Everyone wished Eamonn well but would the back cope with four rigorous days of Open golf on hard, bouncy Birkdale? We know now the back stood up to the punishment but only as a direct result of Darcy having had painful cortisone injections for a spinal problem that had cropped up after he had been drenched in the Cannes Mougins Open two months earlier.

Eamonn Darcy, who has played in every Open since 1976, now lives in Marlow on the River Thames in Buckinghamshire, but comes from Delgany, a village in County Wicklow, south of Dublin.

Delgany is remarkable in that it has produced no fewer than three Ryder Cup players – the late Bradshaw, Jimmy Martin and Darcy, who readily admits he wanted, as a youngster, to be a jockey. The problem was he just grew and grew until a career in horse racing was out of the question. Golf was the alternative.

Hunting and golf are motivating forces in Delgany. When Jim Bradshaw, Harry's brother, retired as club professional at Delgany, it was Eamonn's brother, Martin, who took over and, when Eamonn decides to call it a day as a Tour player, the job will be there for him.

These days most amateurs who turn professional are low handicappers. When Darcy turned pro in 1969, his chances of ending up a winner of twelve titles in places as far apart as New Zealand, Kenya and Europe, and of being a Ryder Cup hero, were somewhat remote. When he joined the paid ranks he had a handicap of twelve and a golf swing that was, to put it at its kindest, idiosyncratic. The swing works for Eamonn, and for no one else, but it works because despite what happens on the back swing, at the top or on the way down, the club head is in perfect position for the hit. That, after all, is what matters.

Darcy, who never had any formal lessons or coaching, but who relies these days on close friend Christy O'Connor, Jr., to occasionally have a look and 'sort out' any little kinks, is sensitive about his swing and cannot quite understand why over the years so many people have made fun of it.

By now, people should realize that Darcy's distinctive 'hoosh' at the ball is going to see him through to the end of his career and there is, after all, a history of unusual Irish styles. Bradshaw had three fingers of the left hand overlapping, Joe Carr gave it a dash, Jimmy Bruen had a loop at the top of the backswing and Fred Daly, the only Irishman to win an Open, in 1947, had a pronounced sway.

One reason put forward as to why Darcy has a swing as distinctive as that of Lee Trevino, Gay Brewer, Miller Barber or Doug Sanders, is how he perfected it, if that is the word, as a youngster at Delgany. He and his pals used to try and hit golf balls over a huge tree at the club – the winner being the fellow who could do so from as close to the tree as possible. Darcy usually won.

Darcy's own view is that the swing just evolved from the raw natural product of no coaching or tuition. Indeed, Watty Sullivan, professional at the Grange Club, once suggested to Eamonn as he watched him play that the one thing he should not do was try to play golf for a living. Darcy did not listen and at Royal Birkdale he became the European Tour's fourteenth millionaire. There is a moral in there somewhere!

It certainly proves that irrespective of the way he swings the club, his constantly repeating action is sound and his determination and competitiveness is finely tuned.

He has thought of making changes, notably after the 1987 Ryder Cup, where he scored a vital point in the first European success on American soil. In the last-day singles, he played Ben Crenshaw who, early in the round, disgusted with his putting, snapped his putter. He used his one iron and wedge after that and did so well he was one up with two holes to play.

Then Darcy struck. Under pressure, he hit a six iron to three feet at the seventeenth and squared the match. Then at the last, where Crenshaw put his drive in a ditch, Darcy came out of a greenside trap and holed a testing left-to-right six-footer downhill for the point. It was a magic moment in Eamonn's career – a moment that underlined his tremendous character and personality.

It was then that Darcy thought about abandoning his eccentric swing for a more orthodox one, but the realization of how long such a radical change would take and with no guarantee that he could handle it, put all thoughts of reconstruction out of his mind.

Eamonn just kept everything the same and avoided any hassle. The amiable big fellow, with a quiet sense of humour, has a relaxed, laid-back attitude. But appearances can be deceptive. His calmness camouflages an inner turmoil. He is a sensitive and very private person. He does worry. He cares.

Darcy does not have a regular caddie. When he turned up at Birkdale, he knew he could recruit someone because there are always plenty of regulars looking for a bag after their own men miss out at the qualifying. Darcy used Mike Clayton's caddie after the Australian did not make it into the final field, aware that Canadian Duncan – Eamonn does not know his last name – and he had teamed up successfully before.

In the first round, Darcy played with Steve Elkington and Chip Beck, and he liked the draw. He had played with Beck before, and knew Elkington to be a pleasant personality. Despite being comfortable with Birkdale, he did not putt particularly well on the first day. He needed thirty-four putts and returned a 78, but one thing Darcy never does is panic and certainly not at the Open.

The Championship does not inspire him, but neither does it overwhelm him. On the second day, the putter worked much better and he shot a 68.

He made his move on the third day when, partnered by Australian Craig Parry, he shot his lowest Open round in the seventeen years he has been playing in it – a 66.

He got off to a really good start on the Saturday, chipping in from the back of the first green for an opening birdie and then making birdies at two of the next four holes, as well. Modestly Darcy describes the round as one 'where the ball was running nicely for me. One where the bounces were all favourable.'

He was the leading European going into the final round and remained so after a closing 68 in which, helped by fifteen-foot birdie putts at the eighth and ninth, he remained in touch with Ian Baker-Finch until the short fourteenth hole. There, he pulled his tee shot and took three more to get down. It was his worst shot of the week, Darcy made no excuses for it.

With only the thought of winning on his mind, Darcy decided that he had no need now for caution. He hit a booming drive on the bunker-strewn fifteenth and caught the big trap 257 yards down the left. The ball ended up against the lip. He could only splash out but then went for a one iron in the hope of still making the green 240 yards away, and maybe even conjuring up a birdie.

Darcy found the left rough short of the green and it was a bad lie as well. His pitch was still short of the green. Trying to hole his next pitch, he sent the ball scuttling eight feet past the cup and missed the return putt. Down went a two-over-par seven on his card, and his hopes of victory had gone, as Baker-Finch, swinging well and putting well, showed no sign of cracking.

Darcy closed par, birdie, par. It might have been three birdies, but he had given it his best shot, and at the end of the day, had finished as the top European of the twelve who were in the top twenty-five.

Six Americans, six Australians and a Fijian completed the list of golfers in that twenty-five who are guaranteed, if not already qualified for, a place in the 1992 Open Championship at Muirfield.

Darcy, four behind Lyle in 1985, had finished five behind, and never once complained about the greens. Perhaps his reward was the ovation he received as he walked down the last hole. There was a three-minute ovation for him and second-placed Mike Harwood.

Eamonn Darcy had not appreciated until then just how popular he was, or how the crowds had warmed to his attempt to score another major win for Europe, for the folks at Delgany and most of all for himself.

The only thing that disappoints him is that the Open is not at Royal St George's next time. Still he is hoping he will be playing as well as he did this year when the Championship does go back to his favourite course, Royal St George's, in 1993.

Taking only 29 strokes for the first nine holes, Ian Baker-Finch was in control throughout the final round.

DAY

4

BAKER-FINCH: FIRST, AT LAST

BY MICHAEL WILLIAMS

Few would argue that the greatest Open Championship of them all was that in 1977 when, the stage long since cleared of even the remotest other challenger, Tom Watson beat Jack Nicklaus by one stroke at Turnberry. Watson was round in 65 in both the third and fourth rounds, while Nicklaus took 65, 66. Two birdies, both at the eighteenth, Nicklaus from the edge of the green as one final defiant gesture, and Watson from much, much closer, was the perfect seal to an unforgettable event.

Watson established two records that day. The first was that his total of 268 for the seventy-two holes set, as it remains today, the lowest aggregate for the Open Championship, while his final thirty-six holes of 130 was another record.

Now the second of these two achievements was equalled, for as the skies cleared from the west and Royal Birkdale basked in sunlight, so Ian Baker-Finch at last played the leading role he had twice understudied in the championship's last pairing.

That 64 in the third round, even if it did only tie him for the lead with Mark O'Meara, had given him another sight of victory, and he never let it shift from his gaze as, with a 66, he came home by two strokes from his fellow Australian, Mike Harwood, equalling in the process Watson's 130 for the last two rounds.

Baker-Finch, tall, dark and with all the good looks of someone who could have an audition for a Hollywood movie, carved one niche that is very much his own. He is the first champion to have begun his final round with an outward half of 29.

Certainly there have been others, perhaps most famously when Tony Jacklin, in the defence of the title he had won at Royal Lytham in 1969, went out in 29 over the Old Course at St Andrews twelve months later. But that was in the first round.

There has even been a 28, by Denis Durnian in the second round the last time the Open had been held at Birkdale in 1983, but for the emerging champion to break that magic figure of 30 was something that had never been done in any of the four major championships.

It has to be said that if it is going to be done anywhere, Royal Birkdale is the place, for the par going out is 34 and needs, therefore, only five birdies. 'Only' is, nevertheless, hardly the appropriate word when the most treasured prize in the world of golf is at stake.

Yet, in the space of about ninety minutes, Baker-Finch had left the field for dead; his first birdie at the second hole, another at the third, then at the fourth, next at the sixth and again at the seventh.

Poor O'Meara, so hopeful when the day had dawned, could find no such inspiration. He may have stood on the first tee with an equal chance of victory, but by the time he climbed to the eighth tee, he was five behind and the dream was over.

It was not quite over elsewhere, for as Baker-Finch glanced at the scoreboard, so his eye caught a sudden charge by Fred Couples, who had begun the day five behind, but now, after an outward half of 32, mounted a realistic challenge with further birdies at the tenth, eleventh, twelfth and thirteenth holes.

He was now five under par, but, as Baker-Finch knew, the American had two par fives to come and, as a formidably long hitter, it was not inconceivable that Couples might have an eagle at one of them and a birdie at the other.

While all this was going through his mind, Baker-Finch played his first false stroke, a less than positive three wood into one of the right-hand bunkers at the tenth hole and it cost him a stroke.

'It was', he said later, 'the result of the first negative thought that had entered my head. I was thinking to myself that I had better not stuff it from here because you will really cop it.' Not for nothing had he assumed the nickname in some unkind quarters of 'Baker-Flinch'.

No sooner did the warning lights flash than they were extinguished, for it was not until the last hole that Baker-Finch erred again, and by then it did not matter. Couples could not summon even a birdie from those last five holes, and his 64 left him tied third with O'Meara (69), a stroke behind the dogged Harwood, whose 67 made sure that this was Australia's day.

Baker-Finch is the fourth Australian to have won the Open, and he did so on the same course on which Peter Thomson took his fifth and last title in 1965. Thomson's prize was £1,500, whereas Baker-Finch collected £90,000.

Thus, too, Europe's record was maintained of never having produced a winner at Birkdale. Fate plays curious tricks, just as it has at Lytham, where no American professional has ever triumphed. The only American who has is Bobby Jones, but he was an amateur.

It was not an encouraging championship for Europe, Eamonn Darcy, of Ireland, being the leading home player as he finished with a last round of 70 for a share of fifth place with Jodie Mudd, who set a course record of 63, which also equalled the championship record, and another American, Bob Tway (66).

Craig Parry, a third Australian, was eighth with a 68, just ahead of yet another in Greg Norman (66), together with Bernhard Langer (Germany), who had 67, and the man on whom the greatest expectations had been fixed, Severiano Ballesteros, of Spain, whose 71 was, to put it mildly, a disappointment.

No one had arrived on the first tee to a bigger cheer, or before a bigger throng, than Ballesteros. He had talked beforehand of the fear of winning that would stab at the hearts of those who had not been there.

Ballesteros had, but the telltale signs one had detected in some of Ballesteros' last rounds in various tournaments surfaced again. In the short space of the first three holes, it was clear that this would not be his day.

A drive into the rough led to a five at the first hole. He was in trouble again at the second but got away with it, while at the third he dropped another shot with three putts. The second was so short that it could only have been the result of the anxiety he had predicted in others.

'I lost my confidence on the greens,' Ballesteros admitted and, as he cast his eye at the scoreboard and saw what Baker-Finch was doing, he knew only too well that the hunt was over.

Baker-Finch's devastating run began at the second, never the easiest of holes, but reduced now to a drive and six iron after which he holed from twelve feet. At the third, of broadly similar length, but a hole that always plays shorter, he hit a three wood from the tee, a wedge to ten feet and the putt went in again.

At the fourth, the Australian took a three iron from the tee, knocked it to six feet and in went the putt for a two. So there was a hat-trick of birdies, and any butterflies in his stomach were still.

If there was a brief lull at the fifth, always the most vulnerable of the holes on the front nine, Baker-Finch pressed home his advantage at the sixth, where the tee had been moved forward so that it was possible to drive over the cross bunkers.

He had only a seven iron to the green and holed

his putt from six feet. At the short seventh it was a seven iron again, now to fifteen feet, and there was his fifth birdie. Five single putts in seven holes and it was virtually all over, bar the shouting.

That one rather careless drive at the tenth was a reminder to Baker-Finch that he could not relax, but from there on he played, without error, regulation golf with two putts on every hole including the seventeenth where, despite a slightly mis-hit drive, he was able to reach the green with a five-iron second for his one birdie of the inward half.

There was no way that Baker-Finch could lose, but his chance of setting a record for the last thirty-six holes was spoiled when he pushed a little over his drive at the eighteenth and hooked into the rough.

From there, he had no chance of getting up in two, and no sooner had he hit, than he was overrun by the traditional charge of spectators as they flooded the fairway. At length he emerged to a tumultuous reception, but the little pitch and two putts was just a touch anti-climatic, even if the result was the same.

After the tears of joy had been wiped away, Baker-Finch said he found it hard to visualize becoming champion. He had deliberately avoided reading newspapers all week, confining his time away from the course to attending to the needs of family life, such as making breakfast for his small daughter, Hayley, and playing with her in the garden.

He believed that he was not only a better player, but one who was better focused, and not only through the glasses he took to wearing at the time of the 1990 Masters. Someone had once given him a black eye in a bar – which is hard to imagine in one of golf's true gentlemen – and this might have had something to do with his having difficulty in picking out the flagsticks when cast in shadow.

'Today erased all the bad memories,' said Baker-Finch, as he looked back on the disappointment of what had happened at St Andrews in both 1984 and 1990. 'To an Australian, this is the most special event of all, and now I'm in a dream world.'

Baker-Finch said that he had played well for the previous twelve months, even if his only victory had been in the Queensland Open. Only the previous week he had, nevertheless, been close, beaten in a play-off for the New England Classic in America.

'I'm sure everyone who wins a major thinks that it is going to be the first of many,' he mused, 'but now I have got my hands on this jug and I don't care. I am sure it will change my life in lots of ways, but I am not afraid of that. I am a big boy now.'

In part, Baker-Finch put down his success to some talks he had had with a sports psychologist, Bob Rotella, from whom he learned the attitude of trying to hole every shot. 'Since then,' he explained, 'I have never thought of trying to get up and down in two, I am always trying to hole the shot, not just get it near. This is the biggest stumbling block I have overcome.'

His one regret was the eighteenth hole, and not only for the five he took. He felt he had been stampeded by the hurrying spectators even as he drove, and it might have forced him to hook. Then, having done so, 'I did not have a chance to smell the roses until I had battled my way through the crowds.'

In fact there were 200 marshals and fifty police to control the hoards, but even then, there was some jostling of the players. Just as there has been through the years – Watson here at Birkdale in 1983, when he never saw his second shot land; Tony Jacklin at Lytham in 1969 when he lost his shoe; even back to the days of Bobby Jones. It is all part of the Open climax, good natured and one that has never affected the result.

The attendance incidentally was right at 190,000, short of the record 208,680 at St Andrews the previous year, but about 47,000 up on the 142,892 the last time the Open had been played at Birkdale.

Harwood thought the crowds were great and his dogged pursuit of Baker-Finch was typical of a still largely underrated player. He had been a little slow to get his momentum going with a bogey at the sixth hole and not getting a birdie until the eighth, which was followed immediately by another at the ninth.

When he then holed from fifteen feet for a three at the eleventh hole, Harwood began to believe he might still have an outside chance, and he sank an even longer putt at the sixteenth for another birdie. He knew, however, that he needed an eagle at the seventeenth and chose this, of all moments, to hit his worst drive of the championship. He took five

Ian Baker-Finch hits his drive on the last hole and finishes with the hugs (inset) of daughter Hayley and wife Jennie.

Bernhard Langer's final-round 67 boosted him to a share of ninth place.

Greg Norman (above) finished with a 66 for 279. Also on 279, Seve Ballesteros said he lost confidence.

and that was it.

O'Meara was full of praise for Baker-Finch, observing him at close quarters and admiring the manner in which he handled the pressure. 'The way he played on the front side was phenomenal,' he said.

For his own part, O'Meara felt he had played only 'fair' to the turn, and when he began to perk up over the inward half, he was largely frustrated by his putting, though he admitted he was perhaps not getting the ball quite close enough to the hole to give himself a genuine chance.

Mudd, who had a 63, set the first target on 277, though he never for a moment thought it would hold up. 'I was too far back,' he said. Nonetheless, it was a great round and he has now finished fourth and fifth twice in his last three Opens. His inward half of 31 with five birdies and eight altogether, put all the complaints about the unpredictability of the greens into perspective.

Tway's 66 was another finishing flourish, while the amiable Darcy had every reason to be well-satisfied with his highest finish in the Open. He thought a 66, which would have given him a total of 273, might have been difficult to beat, but the four he took at the short fourteenth and then a seven at the fifteenth were irrecoverable.

Here Darcy chose not to play safe with an iron from the tee and went instead with his driver. He found a bunker, and that left him with a one-iron third shot to the green, which missed the green left. He had a horrible lie, fluffed it, and then missed a putt of eight feet.

If this was, therefore, a disappointing championship for the Europeans, there was, nevertheless, one winner, and that was Jim Payne, the British Youths' champion from Lincolnshire, who took the silver medal as the championship's leading amateur.

Payne, far from being over-awed by the company of Jack Nicklaus, was positively inspired as he had a last round of 70 for a seventy-two-hole total of 284, which beat Phil Mickelson, the American Amateur champion, by four strokes.

It was a great moment for him and further enhanced by the fact that he beat Nicklaus by a shot, both in this final round and also in the championship itself. The whole manner of his game, and also his bearing on and off the course, suggests that here is a player to watch in the years ahead.

Nicklaus was most complimentary, and the sight of him joining in the applause, after Payne holed out on the eighteenth green, perhaps said the most.

Mike Harwood needed an eagle on the seventeenth hole, but got a par five, and finished on 67-274.

Mark O'Meara tied for third place after sharing the lead.

Bob Tway's 66 provided a share of fifth place.

Also in third place, Jodie Mudd had a sparkling 63.

With his 64, Fred Couples tied O'Meara for third place.

FOURTH ROUND RESULTS

HOLE	1	2	3	4	5	6	7	8	9	10	11	12	13	14	15	16	17	18	
PAR	4	4	4	3	4	4	3	4	4	4	4	3	4	3	5	4	5	4	TOTAL
Ian Baker-Finch	4	3	3	2	4	3	2	4	4	5	4	3	4	3	5	4	4	5	66-272
Mike Harwood	4	4	4	3	4	5	3	3	3	4	3	3	4	3	5	3	5	4	67-274
Fred Couples	4	4	3	3	3	5	3	3	4	3	3	2	3	3	5	4	5	4	64-275
Mark O'Meara	4	4	4	4	4	4	2	5	4	4	4	3	4	3	4	4	4	4	69-275
Jodie Mudd	4	4	3	3	3	5	2	4	4	3	3	3	3	3	4	4	4	4	63-277
Bob Tway	5	3	3	3	4	4	3	4	3	3	4	3	4	3	4	4	5	4	66-277
Eamonn Darcy	4	4	4	2	4	5	3	3	3	4	4	3	4	4	7	4	4	4	70-277
Craig Parry	3	4	3	3	4	5	4	3	5	4	4	4	4	2	5	4	4	3	68-278
Greg Norman	4	3	4	2	3	4	3	5	5	3	4	3	4	2	4	3	5	5	66-279
Bernhard Langer	4	3	4	3	3	5	2	4	4	4	5	3	3	4	4	4	4	4	67-279
Seve Ballesteros	5	4	5	3	4	4	2	4	4	4	4	3	4	3	4	5	5	4	71-279

HOLE SUMMARY

HOLE	PAR	EAGLES	BIRDIES	PARS	BOGEYS	HIGHER	RANK	AVERAGE
1	4	0	6	69	34	3	2	4.32
2	4	0	18	69	21	4	9	4.10
3	4	0	23	82	7	0	16	3.86
4	3	0	20	68	23	1	10	3.04
5	4	0	17	77	17	1	13	4.03
6	4	0	6	67	35	4	1	4.34
7	3	0	24	72	13	3	14	2.96
8	4	0	13	73	22	4	5	4.15
9	4	0	14	70	26	2	8	4.14
OUT	34	0	141	647	198	22		34.94
10	4	0	19	75	15	3	11	4.05
11	4	0	20	71	19	2	12	4.04
12	3	0	12	77	22	1	7	3.11
13	4	0	7	85	16	4	5	4.15
14	3	0	16	88	8	0	15	2.93
15	5	1	38	59	11	3	17	4.79
16	4	0	11	71	24	6	3	4.24
17	5	6	76	24	4	2	18	4.29
18	4	0	6	77	25	4	3	4.24
IN	36	7	205	627	144	25		35.84
TOTAL	70	7	346	1274	342	47		70.78

Players Below Par	36
Players At Par	16
Players Above Par	60

LOW SCORES		
Low First Nine	Ian Baker-Finch	29
Low Second Nine	Jodie Mudd	31
Low Round	Jodie Mudd	63

CHAMPIONSHIP HOLE SUMMARY

HOLE	PAR	EAGLES	BIRDIES	PARS	BOGEYS	HIGHER	RANK	AVERAGE
1	4	0	36	295	186	20	3	4.36
2	4	0	54	299	159	25	4	4.29
3	4	1	92	400	43	1	17	3.91
4	3	0	67	361	103	6	12	3.09
5	4	0	78	357	93	9	14	4.07
6	4	0	18	235	243	41	1	4.59
7	3	0	90	347	91	9	15	3.04
8	4	1	58	380	90	8	13	4.09
9	4	0	69	339	110	18	8	4.15
OUT	**34**	**2**	**562**	**3013**	**1118**	**137**		**35.59**
10	4	0	63	355	105	13	10	4.14
11	4	0	63	329	123	21	7	4.20
12	3	1	56	335	133	11	6	3.18
13	4	0	59	362	100	15	11	4.13
14	3	0	53	379	97	7	9	3.11
15	5	2	114	319	90	11	16	4.99
16	4	0	42	296	165	33	2	4.37
17	5	38	357	128	11	2	18	4.22
18	4	0	40	336	135	24	5	4.27
IN	**36**	**41**	**847**	**2839**	**959**	**137**		**36.61**
TOTAL	**70**	**43**	**1409**	**5852**	**2077**	**274**		**72.20**

	FIRST ROUND	SECOND ROUND	THIRD ROUND	FOURTH ROUND	TOTAL
Players Below Par	17	19	30	36	102
Players At Par	11	8	17	16	52
Players Above Par	128	128	65	60	381

ATTENDANCE

PRACTICE ROUNDS	34,848
FIRST ROUND	34,417
SECOND ROUND	43,601
THIRD ROUND	40,069
FOURTH ROUND	36,500
TOTAL	189,435

Daughter Hayley shared Ian Baker-Finch's joy in winning the Open Championship.

THE RISE OF IAN BAKER-FINCH

BY JOHN HOPKINS

Ian Baker-Finch first made a significant impression on me at St Andrews in 1984. I might have been aware of him in the odd tournament on the European Tour prior to that, but only fleetingly. At that time, 1983, Nick Faldo was cutting a wide swathe, winning five tournaments, three in a row; Greg Norman was the dominant Australian; and Seve Ballesteros, with two Masters titles and one Open Championship, was the presiding genius of the entire circuit.

All that changed in the Open seven summers ago. Baker-Finch started with a 68, one stroke behind the leaders, and the Press likened him to the hares who race to the front at the start of the Open and then fall back from that moment on.

We expected Ian Baker-Finch to do the same. He did not. He added a second round of 66 to take the outright lead. At that point we started to pay attention and began roaming the broad fields of our memories to see what we could come up with about him.

There hadn't been many hyphenated golfers, and none from Australia as far as we could ascertain. One reporter on a Scottish paper wrote that he sounded like a character out of P. G. Wodehouse. Herbert Warren Wind took the same theme and wrote it better in the *New Yorker*, as you would expect from a man who had written a long essay (later turned into a book) on P. G. Wodehouse: 'All the good P. G. Wodehouse fans, who appreciate the kind of double-barrelled name one would run into at the Drones Club, immediately announced they would be supporting this Baker-Finch chap . . .'

To me he seemed to step from the John Betjeman poem entitled 'A subaltern's love-song,' in which the central figure is one Miss Joan Hunter Dunn, 'furnish'd and burnish'd by Aldershot sun . . .' I associated him with pink because that was the colour he wore when I first saw him. Not many Australians wear pink. Not many Englishmen do for that matter. It is not considered a masculine colour, and it takes a man of considerable self confidence to wear it. Clearly Baker-Finch had this in abundance. He was tall, dark and plumpishly, boyishly handsome. He spoke quietly, had a ready smile and he didn't seem to be as rough-edged as many Aussies.

And he could play golf. He had been brought along by the wiliest of Australian players, Peter Thomson, who had forecast great things for him. From time to time, Kel Nagle, who won the Centenary Open at St Andrews in 1960, added a little extra polish. Just one of many aspects of Baker-Finch that marked him out from the run of the mill golfers was his swing. At a time when short, functional swings were a la mode, Baker-Finch's was long and languid, reminiscent of Sam Snead's and Faldo's.

In interviews, Baker-Finch seemed as assured in talking about himself as he obviously was on the golf course. 'I'm not surprised to be leading,' he said, reminding us that he had won a New Zealand Open and a West Australian Open. 'But I would be surprised to win this.'

Baker-Finch was born on 24 October 1960, in Peachester, Queensland, a hamlet comprising a few houses, a general store, a petrol station and a post office. His parents owned a farm on which they reared poultry and grew avocados. Later, his father turned the family ranch in to a stud piggery.

All Australians seem to be keen on sport of some sort or another, and Baker-Finch was no exception. He was interested in cricket, tennis and rugby, but from the moment he received a half set of golf clubs on his twelfth birthday, golf took precedence over everything. Within one year he had a handicap of thirteen. By the time he was fifteen years old, he had decided to become a pro. 'There was no question of my staying on for further education,' he said. 'Only rocket scientists did that.'

About the same time there were Australians of similar age growing up in other parts of Australia, and their rivalry spurred one another on in the way that Ballesteros, Bernhard Langer, Sandy Lyle, Faldo and Ian Woosnam were to do so in Europe. Norman was the best, but there were also Peter Senior, Wayne Grady and a tall young man named Mike Harwood. 'We were all from simple beginnings. We played where we could, when we could,' said Baker-Finch. 'We started with nothing and we made it. It's a nice feeling. When you see one person do well, you think that if he can do it, so can I. You feed off each other's success.'

'We all grew up on the Sunshine Tour in Australia,' Harwood said. 'I used to kick his arse (Baker-Finch's) then. I would play well for two days; he would play well for four days. He was always very aggressive. In the early days he would shoot a 64 and then follow it with a 78 but now he has settled down.'

In the third round at St Andrews in 1984, Baker-Finch was paired with Faldo. Two tall young men together and it was assumed that Baker-Finch, who was leading by three strokes, would begin to fold under the unaccustomed pressure. Just as we were wrong in expecting him to disappear after his good first round, so we were wrong now. It was Faldo who wilted, scoring a 76. This was one of the bad rounds in major championships that convinced him he needed to remodel his swing to make it withstand pressure better. Baker-Finch's score was a 71. His prize was to be paired with Tom Watson in the last pair on the final day, and this was when he finally showed his inexperience. From the moment his second shot to the first hole spun back into the Swilcan Burn, he was under pressure. He took 41 strokes to reach the turn and ended in 79 and a tie for ninth.

'I had to fight to keep the tears out of my eyes,' he recalled years later. 'For me it was a dream come true to play the final round with Watson, but it was difficult. I was so apprehensive. I got so many over par. You start feeling a lot of emotion out there. You start feeling like you screwed up and you're wondering what everyone is thinking. And you're thinking that the whole of Australia is sitting up watching you shoot 79. I felt I had failed. But after a week, I realised that just because you fail, it doesn't make you a failure.'

Two things stick in the mind, however, about Baker-Finch's performance on that fourth day at St Andrews. He played the last four holes of the championship in two under par, birdie, par, par and birdie. This was an impressive finish and suggested that we hadn't seen the last of the tall man with the hyphen.

What also bode well for the future, was the rousing farewell given to him by the crowd outside the R&A clubhouse as he headed south. Being knowledgeable Scots golfers, they knew they had seen something in him that made them mark him down as a man to watch in the coming years.

They got the chance to reacquaint themselves with Baker-Finch when he returned for the 119th Open. The boyish young man who had been so popular in 1984 had matured. His plump face with its fresh look, which contributed to his nickname of Peachy, had firmed up. No rocket scientist, he remained the smiling, quietly-spoken and personable Australian he had been six years earlier, except he had grown into a battle-hardened competitor, one forged on the anvil of the American tour. He had won three tournaments in Japan in 1988, nearly won the World Series of Golf and decided he was good enough to try his luck on the US tour. In 1989, his first full year, he won the Colonial Invitational in Texas.

In his pursuit of success, he was helped by the competitiveness of his countrymen, the same men with whom he had struggled ten years earlier. Again, Norman was the front runner. After winning the Open at Turnberry in 1986, he had rarely slipped from his position of number one in the Sony world rankings. Baker-Finch, Grady, Steve Elkington, Senior, Craig Parry and Rodger Davis all sought to emulate him, and this spurred each of them to heights they might not have reached otherwise.

In 1990, Baker-Finch was suffering from limited vision in his right eye. At the Masters a couple of months earlier, he had started wearing glasses, almost certainly the result of a punch he had taken in a bar brawl in Australia a year or two earlier when a drunk, whose girlfriend was taking rather too close an interest in Baker-Finch, had punched him.

In some ways, 1990 at St Andrews was 1984 all over again, an essential lesson in the Baker-Finch learning process. After rounds of 68, 72 and 64, Baker-Finch found himself in the last pairing in the final round. This time his partner was Faldo, the reigning Masters champion and holder of two other major titles as well. Baker-Finch shot a 73, two worse than Faldo and finished joint sixth.

'Nick didn't say a word to me all the way round,' said Baker-Finch. 'But that didn't matter. He was truly absorbed in what he was doing. He was being very professional. I was playing as well as I could and I let things bother me. Nick was focused on his job and I was just a marker by his side. He knew what he had to do and he did it well. Early in the round it was the procession, all the buggys and the dust, going on ahead of me that bothered me. It didn't worry Nick. He went about his work and concentrated and did not worry about that. I learned a lot that day.'

'I will remember 1984 for the pain, and 1990 for the experience,' Baker-Finch said after the third round, another 64, at Royal Birkdale a year later. 'I am definitely tougher and more prepared now. In 1984, I was just a little kid with starry eyes having a great time. Last year, I was a little bigger and I learned a lot from Faldo. I have improved since then and have a lot to thank Nick for. I learned I needed to be more focused on what I was going to do and not allow outside influences to upset me. I knew that, but sometimes you need a kick in the pants to jog the memory.'

What he had learned in 1984 and 1990, he was able to put to good use at Royal Birkdale when, for the third time in seven years, he was in the last pairing on the final day. He knew there were serious questions he had to answer: had he learned the lessons of 1984 and 1990? Both Watson and Faldo had thrown away similar chances to win major championships because they weren't mature enough to take them. You could do this twice, as they had, but then you had to win the third time, otherwise there might not be another chance. Was Baker-Finch ready to win his first major championship? He had the tools; could he get the job done?

Baker-Finch answered the questions so emphatically, he threatened to run away with the Open with a roaring start of five birdies in seven holes. It gave him a lead of five strokes at one point. You knew then he was going to win; it was merely a question of by how many. 'When I was four and five under I thought to myself, you'd better not stuff it up from here or you'll really cop it,' he said.

He didn't stuff it up. He played near faultless golf, the only blemishes coming on the tenth, where he tried to be too casual with a three wood and hit it into the first of the two bunkers on the right of the fairway, and the eighteenth, where he was distracted by the rushing spectators all around him. For the rest of a warm, sunny afternoon he was serenity itself.

His last round of 66, which with his 64 the previous day meant that he had played the two closing rounds in ten under par, were worth a lot to him. They proved that he could demonstrate grace under pressure in Kipling's phrase. More importantly, they announced that a new star had arrived in the world of golf. His apprenticeship had been long and public. It was over now.

Champion Ian Baker-Finch said, 'I feel on top of the world today . . . I'm in a dream world right now.'

120th
CHAMPIONSHIP
1991
ROYAL BIRKDALE
GOLF CLUB
SCORE
PLAYER
POSITION AFTER 53 HOLES
SCORE FOR ROUND
GAME NO 46
ROCCA
GAME NO 44
ALLAN
NO CLIMBING ON STANDS PLEASE

Baker-Finch is perhaps the best putter in the world and a relentlessly straight driver. He has the equipment to go on and win more major titles if he wants to. The question is not whether he is too nice to win, because he has won often enough. The question is whether the fire burns fiercely enough for him to want to carry on winning. He has proved that nice guys can finish first, as Grady did in the 1990 U.S. PGA Championship. But nice guys finish last, too, and Baker-Finch had better not forget that.

Ian Baker-Finch was swinging well, and with great confidence.

Caddie Pete Bender was with an Open champion for the second time. Bender caddied for Greg Norman in 1986.

Tom Watson, Open champion in 1975, 1977, 1980, 1982 and 1983.

RECORDS OF THE OPEN CHAMPIONSHIP

MOST VICTORIES
6, Harry Vardon, 1896-98-99-1903-11-14
5, James Braid, 1901-05-06-08-10; J.H. Taylor, 1894-95-1900-09-13; Peter Thomson, 1954-55-56-58-65; Tom Watson, 1975-77-80-82-83

MOST TIMES RUNNER-UP OR JOINT RUNNER-UP
7, Jack Nicklaus, 1964-67-68-72-76-77-79
6, J.H. Taylor, 1896-1904-05-06-07-14

OLDEST WINNER
Old Tom Morris, 46 years 99 days, 1867
Roberto de Vicenzo, 44 years 93 days, 1967

YOUNGEST WINNER
Young Tom Morris, 17 years 5 months 8 days, 1868
Willie Auchterlonie, 21 years 24 days, 1893
Severiano Ballesteros, 22 years 3 months 12 days, 1979

YOUNGEST AND OLDEST COMPETITOR
John Ball, 14 years, 1878
Gene Sarazen, 71 years 4 months 13 days, 1973

BIGGEST MARGIN OF VICTORY
13 strokes, Old Tom Morris, 1862
12 strokes, Young Tom Morris, 1870
8 strokes, J.H. Taylor, 1900 and 1913; James Braid, 1908
6 strokes, Bobby Jones, 1927; Walter Hagen, 1929; Arnold Palmer, 1962; Johnny Miller, 1976

LOWEST WINNING AGGREGATES
268 (68, 70, 65, 65), Tom Watson, Turnberry, 1977
270 (67, 65, 67, 71), Nick Faldo, St Andrews, 1990
271 (68, 70, 64, 69), Tom Watson, Muirfield, 1980
272 (71, 71, 64, 66), Ian Baker-Finch, Royal Birkdale, 1991

LOWEST AGGREGATES BY RUNNER-UP
269 (68, 70, 65, 66), Jack Nicklaus, Turnberry, 1977
274 (68, 70, 69, 67), Mike Harwood, Royal Birkdale, 1991
275 (68, 67, 71, 69), Lee Trevino, Muirfield, 1980
275 (70, 67, 69, 69), Nick Price, Royal Lytham, 1988
275 (69, 70, 72, 64), Greg Norman, Royal Troon, 1989
275 (68, 67, 69, 71), Wayne Grady, Royal Troon, 1989
275 (74, 68, 68, 65), Mark McNulty, St Andrews, 1990
275 (68, 68, 68, 71), Payne Stewart, St Andrews, 1990

LOWEST AGGREGATE BY AN AMATEUR
283 (74, 70, 71, 68), Guy Wolstenholme, St Andrews, 1960

LOWEST INDIVIDUAL ROUND
63, Mark Hayes, second round, Turnberry, 1977; Isao Aoki, third round, Muirfield, 1980; Greg Norman, second round, Turnberry, 1986; Paul Broadhurst, third round, St Andrews, 1990

LOWEST INDIVIDUAL ROUND BY AN AMATEUR
66, Frank Stranahan, fourth round, Troon, 1950

LOWEST FIRST ROUND
64, Craig Stadler, Royal Birkdale, 1983; Christy O'Connor Jr., Royal St George's, 1985; Rodger Davis, Muirfield, 1987

LOWEST SECOND ROUND
63, Mark Hayes, Turnberry, 1977; Greg Norman, Turnberry, 1986

LOWEST THIRD ROUND
63, Isao Aoki, Muirfield, 1980; Paul Broadhurst, St Andrews, 1990

LOWEST FOURTH ROUND
63, Jodie Mudd, Royal Birkdale, 1991

LOWEST FIRST 36 HOLES
132 (67, 65) Henry Cotton, Sandwich, 1934; (66, 66) Greg Norman and (67,65) Nick Faldo, St Andrews, 1990

LOWEST SECOND 36 HOLES
130 (65, 65), Tom Watson, Turnberry, 1977; (64, 66) Ian Baker-Finch, Royal Birkdale, 1991

LOWEST FIRST 54 HOLES
199 (67, 65, 67), Nick Faldo, St Andrews, 1990
202 (68, 70, 64), Tom Watson, Muirfield, 1980

LOWEST FINAL 54 HOLES
200 (70, 65, 65), Tom Watson, Turnberry, 1977
201 (71, 64, 66), Ian Baker-Finch, Royal Birkdale, 1991

LOWEST 9 HOLES
28, Denis Durnian, first 9, Royal Birkdale, 1983
29, Peter Thomson and Tom Haliburton, first 9, Royal

Lytham, 1958; Tony Jacklin, first 9, St Andrews, 1970; Bill Longmuir, first 9, Royal Lytham, 1979; David J. Russell, first 9, Royal Lytham, 1988; Ian Baker-Finch and Paul Broadhurst, first 9, St Andrews, 1990; Ian Baker-Finch, first 9, Royal Birkdale, 1991

CHAMPIONS IN THREE DECADES
Harry Vardon, 1896, 1903, 1911
J.H. Taylor, 1894, 1900, 1913
Gary Player, 1959, 1968, 1974

BIGGEST SPAN BETWEEN FIRST AND LAST VICTORIES
19 years, J.H. Taylor, 1894-1913
18 years, Harry Vardon, 1896-1914
15 years, Gary Player, 1959-74
14 years, Henry Cotton, 1934-48

SUCCESSIVE VICTORIES
4, Young Tom Morris, 1868-72. No championship in 1871
3, Jamie Anderson, 1877-79; Bob Ferguson, 1880-82, Peter Thomson, 1954-56
2, Old Tom Morris, 1861-62; J.H. Taylor, 1894-95; Harry Vardon, 1898-99; James Braid, 1905-06; Bobby Jones, 1926-27; Walter Hagen, 1928-29; Bobby Locke, 1949-50; Arnold Palmer, 1961-62; Lee Trevino, 1971-72; Tom Watson, 1982-83

VICTORIES BY AMATEURS
3, Bobby Jones, 1926-27-30
2, Harold Hilton, 1892-97
1, John Ball, 1890
Roger Wethered lost a play-off in 1921

HIGHEST NUMBER OF TOP FIVE FINISHES
16, J.H. Taylor, Jack Nicklaus
15, Harry Vardon, James Braid

HIGHEST NUMBER OF ROUNDS UNDER 70
30, Jack Nicklaus
23, Tom Watson
21, Nick Faldo
20, Lee Trevino
16, Severiano Ballesteros
15, Peter Thomson
14, Gary Player
13, Ben Crenshaw, Bernhard Langer
12, Bobby Locke, Arnold Palmer, Greg Norman
11, Payne Stewart

OUTRIGHT LEADER AFTER EVERY ROUND
Willie Auchterlonie, 1893; J.H. Taylor, 1894 and 1900; James Braid, 1908; Ted Ray, 1912; Bobby Jones, 1927; Gene Sarazen, 1932; Henry Cotton, 1934; Tom Weiskopf, 1973

RECORD LEADS (SINCE 1892)
After 18 holes:
4 strokes, James Braid, 1908; Bobby Jones, 1927; Henry Cotton, 1934; Christy O'Connor Jr., 1985
After 36 holes:
9 strokes, Henry Cotton, 1934
After 54 holes:
10 strokes, Henry Cotton, 1934
7 strokes, Tony Lema, 1964
6 strokes, James Braid, 1908
5 strokes, Arnold Palmer, 1962; Bill Rogers, 1981; Nick Faldo, 1990

CHAMPIONS WITH EACH ROUND LOWER THAN PREVIOUS ONE
Jack White, 1904, Sandwich, 80, 75, 72, 69
James Braid, 1906, Muirfield, 77, 76, 74, 73
Ben Hogan, 1953, Carnoustie, 73, 71, 70, 68
Gary Player, 1959, Muirfield, 75, 71, 70, 68

CHAMPION WITH FOUR ROUNDS THE SAME
Densmore Shute, 1933, St Andrews, 73, 73, 73, 73 (excluding the play-off)

BIGGEST VARIATION BETWEEN ROUNDS OF A CHAMPION
14 strokes, Henry Cotton, 1934, second round 65, fourth round 79
11 strokes, Jack White, 1904, first round 80, fourth round 69, Greg Norman, 1986, first round 74, second round 63, third round 74

BIGGEST VARIATION BETWEEN TWO ROUNDS
17 strokes, Jack Nicklaus, 1981, first round 83, second round 66; Ian Baker-Finch, 1986, first round 86, second round 69

BEST COMEBACK BY CHAMPIONS
After 18 holes:
Harry Vardon, 1896, 11 strokes behind the leader
After 36 holes:
George Duncan, 1920, 13 strokes behind the leader
After 54 holes:
Jim Barnes, 1925, 5 strokes behind the leader
Of non-champions, Greg Norman, 1989, 7 strokes behind the leader and lost in a play-off

CHAMPIONS WITH FOUR ROUNDS UNDER 70
None
Arnold Palmer, 1962, Tom Watson, 1977 and 1980, Severiano Ballesteros, 1984, Mark Calcavecchia, 1989, and Nick Faldo, 1990, had three rounds under 70
Of non-champions, Phil Rodgers, 1963, Jack Nicklaus, 1977, Lee Trevino, 1980, Nick Faldo, 1984, Nick Price and Curtis Strange, 1988, Wayne Grady and Tom Watson, 1989, Mark McNulty, Payne Stewart, Ian Woosnam and Greg Norman, 1990, Mike Harwood and Mark O'Meara, 1991, had three rounds under 70

BEST FINISHING ROUND BY A CHAMPION
65, Tom Watson, Turnberry, 1977; Severiano Ballesteros, Royal Lytham, 1988
66, Johnny Miller, Royal Birkdale, 1976; Ian Baker-Finch, Royal Birkdale, 1991

WORST FINISHING ROUND BY A CHAMPION SINCE 1920
79, Henry Cotton, Sandwich, 1934
78, Reg Whitcombe, Sandwich, 1938
77, Walter Hagen, Hoylake, 1924

WORST OPENING ROUND BY A CHAMPION SINCE 1919
80, George Duncan, Deal, 1920 (he also had a second round of 80)
77, Walter Hagen, Hoylake, 1924

BEST OPENING ROUND BY A CHAMPION
66, Peter Thomson, Royal Lytham, 1958
67, Henry Cotton, Sandwich, 1934; Tom Watson, Royal Birkdale, 1983; Severiano Ballesteros, Royal Lytham, 1988; Nick Faldo, St Andrews, 1990

BIGGEST RECOVERY IN 18 HOLES BY A CHAMPION
George Duncan, Deal, 1920, was 13 strokes behind the leader, Abe Mitchell, after 36 holes and level after 54

MOST APPEARANCES ON FINAL DAY (SINCE 1892)
30, J.H. Taylor
29, Jack Nicklaus
27, Harry Vardon, James Braid
26, Peter Thomson
25, Gary Player
23, Dai Rees
22, Henry Cotton

CHAMPIONSHIP WITH HIGHEST NUMBER OF ROUNDS UNDER 70
102, Royal Birkdale, 1991

CHAMPIONSHIP SINCE 1946 WITH THE FEWEST ROUNDS UNDER 70
St Andrews, 1946; Hoylake, 1947; Portrush, 1951; Hoylake, 1956; Carnoustie, 1968. All had only two rounds under 70

LONGEST COURSE
Carnoustie, 1968, 7252 yd (6631 m)

COURSES MOST OFTEN USED
St Andrews and Prestwick, (but not since 1925), 24; Muirfield, 13; Sandwich, 11; Hoylake, 10; Royal Lytham, 8; Royal Birkdale, 7; Musselburgh, and Royal Troon, 6; Carnoustie, 5; Deal and Turnberry, 2; Royal Portrush and Prince's, 1

PRIZE MONEY

Year	*Total*	*First Prize*
1860	nil	nil
1863	10	nil
1864	16	6
1876	20	20
1889	22	8
1891	28.50	10
1892	110	(Amateur winner)
1893	100	30
1910	125	50
1920	225	75
1927	275	100
1930	400	100
1931	500	100
1946	1,000	150
1949	1,700	300
1953	2,450	500
1954	3,500	750
1955	3,750	1,000
1958	4,850	1,000
1959	5,000	1,000
1960	7,000	1,250
1961	8,500	1,400
1963	8,500	1,500
1965	10,000	1,750
1966	15,000	2,100
1968	20,000	3,000
1969	30,000	4,250
1970	40,000	5,250
1971	45,000	5,500
1972	50,000	5,500
1975	75,000	7,500
1977	100,000	10,000
1978	125,000	12,500
1979	155,000	15,500
1980	200,000	25,000
1982	250,000	32,000
1983	300,000	40,000
1984	451,000	55,000
1985	530,000	65,000
1986	600,000	70,000
1987	650,000	75,000
1988	700,000	80,000
1989	750,000	80,000
1990	825,000	85,000
1991	900,000	90,000

ATTENDANCE

Year	*Attendance*
1962	37,098
1963	24,585
1964	35,954
1965	32,927
1966	40,182
1967	29,880
1968	51,819
1969	46,001
1970	81,593
1971	70,076
1972	84,746
1973	78,810
1974	92,796
1975	85,258
1976	92,021
1977	87,615
1978	125,271
1979	134,501
1980	131,610
1981	111,987
1982	133,299
1983	142,892
1984	193,126
1985	141,619
1986	134,261
1987	139,189
1988	191,334
1989	160,639
1990	208,680
1991	189,435

Tom Weiskopf (above left), 1973 champion. Gary Player (above), 1959, 1968 and 1974 champion. Johnny Miller (left), 1976 champion.

Jack Nicklaus, 1966, 1970 and 1978 champion.

PAST RESULTS

* Denotes amateurs

1860 PRESTWICK

Willie Park, Musselburgh	55	59	60	174
Tom Morris Sr, Prestwick	58	59	59	176
Andrew Strath, St Andrews				180
Robert Andrew, Perth				191
George Brown, Blackheath				192
Charles Hunter, Prestwick St Nicholas				195

1861 PRESTWICK

Tom Morris Sr, Prestwick	54	56	53	163
Willie Park, Musselburgh	54	54	59	167
William Dow, Musselburgh	59	58	54	171
David Park, Musselburgh	58	57	57	172
Robert Andrew, Perth	58	61	56	175
Peter McEwan, Bruntsfield	56	60	62	178

1862 PRESTWICK

Tom Morris Sr, Prestwick	52	55	56	163
Willie Park, Musselburgh	59	59	58	176
Charles Hunter, Prestwick	60	60	58	178
William Dow, Musselburgh	60	58	63	181
* James Knight, Prestwick	62	61	63	186
* J.F. Johnston, Prestwick	64	69	75	208

1863 PRESTWICK

Willie Park, Musselburgh	56	54	58	168
Tom Morris Sr, Prestwick	56	58	56	170
David Park, Musselburgh	55	63	54	172
Andrew Strath, St Andrews	61	55	58	174
George Brown, St Andrews	58	61	57	176
Robert Andrew, Perth	62	57	59	178

1864 PRESTWICK

Tom Morris Sr, Prestwick	54	58	55	167
Andrew Strath, St Andrews	56	57	56	169
Robert Andrew, Perth	57	58	60	175
Willie Park, Musselburgh	55	67	55	177
William Dow, Musselburgh	56	58	67	181
William Strath, St Andrews	60	62	60	182

1865 PRESTWICK

Andrew Strath, St Andrews	55	54	53	162
Willie Park, Musselburgh	56	52	56	164
William Dow, Musselburgh				171
Robert Kirk, St Andrews	64	54	55	173
Tom Morris Sr, St Andrews	57	61	56	174
*William Doleman, Glasgow	62	57	59	178

1866 PRESTWICK

Willie Park, Musselburgh	54	56	59	169
David Park, Musselburgh	58	57	56	171
Robert Andrew, Perth	58	59	59	176
Tom Morris Sr, St Andrews	61	58	59	178
Robert Kirk, St Andrews	60	62	58	180
Andrew Strath, Prestwick	61	61	60	182
* William Doleman, Glasgow	60	60	62	182

1867 PRESTWICK

Tom Morris, St Andrews	58	54	58	170
Willie Park, Musselburgh	58	56	58	172
Andrew Strath, St Andrews	61	57	56	174
Tom Morris Jr, St Andrews	58	59	58	175
Robert Kirk, St Andrews	57	60	60	177
*William Doleman, Glasgow	55	66	57	178

1868 PRESTWICK

Tom Morris Jr, St Andrews	50	55	52	157
Robert Andrew, Perth	53	54	52	159
Willie Park, Musselburgh	58	50	54	162
Robert Kirk, St Andrews	56	59	56	171
John Allen, Westward Ho!	54	52	63	172
Tom Morris St, St Andrews	56	62	58	176

1869 PRESTWICK

Tom Morris Jr, St Andrews	51	54	49	154
Tom Morris Sr, St Andrews	54	50	53	157
* S. Mure Fergusson, Royal and Ancient	57	54	54	165
Robert Kirk, St Andrews	53	58	57	168
David Strath, St Andrews	53	56	60	169
Jamie Anderson, St Andrews	60	56	57	173

1870 PRESTWICK

Tom Morris Jr, St Andrews	47	51	51	149
Bob Kirk, Royal Blackheath	52	52	57	161
David Strath, St Andrews	54	49	58	161
Tom Morris Sr, St Andrews	56	52	54	162
* William Doleman, Musselburgh	57	56	58	171
Willie Park, Musselburgh	60	55	58	173

1871 NO COMPETITION

1872 PRESTWICK

Tom Morris Jr, St Andrews	57	56	53	166
David Strath, St Andrews	56	52	61	169
* William Doleman, Musselburgh	63	60	54	177
Tom Morris Sr, St Andrews	62	60	57	179
David Park, Musselburgh	61	57	61	179
Charlie Hunter, Prestwick	60	60	69	189

1873 ST ANDREWS

Tom Kidd, St Andrews	91	88	179
Jamie Anderson, St Andrews	91	89	180
Tom Morris Jr, St Andrews	94	89	183
Bob Kirk, Royal Blackheath	91	92	183
David Strath, St Andrews	97	90	187
Walter Gourlay, St Andrews	92	96	188

1874 MUSSELBURGH

Mungo Park, Musselburgh	75	84	159
Tom Morris Jr, St Andrews	83	78	161
George Paxton, Musselburgh	80	82	162
Bob Martin, St Andrews	85	79	164
Jamie Anderson, St Andrews	82	83	165
David Park, Musselburgh	83	83	166
W. Thomson, Edinburgh	84	82	166

1875 PRESTWICK

Willie Park, Musselburgh	56	59	51	166
Bob Martin, St Andrews	56	58	54	168
Mungo Park, Musselburgh	59	57	55	171
Robert Ferguson, Musselburgh	58	56	58	172
James Rennie, St Andrews	61	59	57	177
David Strath, St Andrews	59	61	58	178

1876 ST ANDREWS

Bob Martin, St Andrews	86	90	176
David Strath, North Berwick	86	90	176
(Martin was awarded the title when Strath refused to play-off)			
Willie Park, Musselburgh	94	89	183
Tom Morris Sr, St Andrews	90	95	185
W. Thomson, Elie	90	95	185
Mungo Park, Musselburgh	95	90	185

1877 MUSSELBURGH

Jamie Anderson, St Andrews	40	42	37	41	160
Bob Pringle, Musselburgh	44	38	40	40	162
Bob Ferguson, Musselburgh	40	40	40	44	164
William Cosgrove, Musselburgh	41	39	44	40	164
David Strath, North Berwick	45	40	38	43	166
William Brown, Musselburgh	39	41	45	41	166

1878 PRESTWICK

Jamie Anderson, St Andrews	53	53	51	157
Bob Kirk, St Andrews	53	55	51	159
J.O.F. Morris, St Andrews	50	56	55	61
Bob Martin, St Andrews	57	53	55	165
*John Ball, Hoylake	53	57	55	165
Willie Park, Musselburgh	53	56	57	166
William Cosgrove, Musselburgh	53	56	55	166

1879 ST ANDREWS

Jamie Anderson, St Andrews	84	85	169
James Allan, Westward Ho!	88	84	172
Andrew Kirkaldy, St Andrews	86	86	172
George Paxton, Musselburgh			174
Tom Kidd, St Andrews			175
Bob Ferguson, Musselburgh			176

1880 MUSSELBURGH

Bob Ferguson, Musselburgh	81	81	162
Peter Paxton, Musselburgh	81	86	167
Ned Cosgrove, Musselburgh	82	86	168
George Paxton, Musselburgh	85	84	169
Bob Pringle, Musselburgh	90	79	169
David Brown, Musselburgh	86	83	169

1881 PRESTWICK

Bob Ferguson, Musselburgh	53	60	57	170
Jamie Anderson, St Andrews	57	60	56	73
Ned Cosgrove, Musselburgh	61	59	57	177
Bob Martin, St Andrews	57	62	59	178
Tom Morris Sr, St Andrews	58	65	58	181
Willie Campbell, Musselburgh	60	56	65	181
Willie Park Jr, Musselburgh	66	57	58	81

1882 ST ANDREWS

Bob Ferguson, Musselburgh	83	88	171
Willie Fernie, Dumfries	88	86	174
Jamie Anderson, St Andrews	87	88	175
John Kirkaldy, St Andrews	86	89	175
Bob Martin, St Andrews	89	86	175
*Fitz Boothby, St Andrews	86	89	175

1883 MUSSELBURGH

Willie Fernie, Dumfries	75	84	159
Bob Ferguson, Musselburgh	78	80	159
(Fernie won play-off 158 to 159)			
William Brown, Musselburgh	83	77	160
Bob Pringle, Musselburgh	79	82	161
Willie Campbell, Musselburgh	80	83	163
George Paxton, Musselburgh	80	83	163

1884 PRESTWICK

Jack Simpson, Carnoustie	78	82	160
David Rollan, Elie	81	83	164
Willie Fernie, Felixstowe	80	84	164
Willie Campbell, Musselburgh	84	85	169
Willie Park Jr, Musselburgh	86	83	169
Ben Sayers, North Berwick	83	87	170

1885 ST ANDREWS

Bob Martin, St Andrews	84	87	171
Archie Simpson, Carnoustie	83	89	172
David Ayton, St Andrews	89	84	173
Willie Fernie, Felixstowe	89	85	174
Willie Park Jr, Musselburgh	86	88	174
Bob Simpson, Carnoustie	85	89	174

1886 MUSSELBURGH

David Brown, Musselburgh	79	78	157
Willie Campbell, Musselburgh	78	81	159
Ben Campbell, Musselburgh	79	81	160
Archie Simpson, Carnoustie	82	79	161
Willie Park Jr, Musselburgh	84	77	161
Thomas Gossett, Musselburgh	82	79	161
Bob Ferguson, Musselburgh	82	79	161

1887 PRESTWICK

Willie Park Jr, Musselburgh	82	79	161
Bob Martin, St Andrews	81	81	162
Willie Campbell, Prestwick	77	87	164
*Johnny Laidlay, Honourable Company	86	80	166
Ben Sayers, North Berwick	83	85	168
Archie Simpson, Carnoustie	81	87	168

1888 ST ANDREWS

Jack Burns, Warwick	86	85	171
David Anderson Jr, St Andrews	86	86	172
Ben Sayers, North Berwick	85	87	172
Willie Campbell, Prestwick	84	90	174
* Leslie Balfour, Edinburgh	86	89	175
Andrew Kirkaldy, St Andrews	87	89	176
David Grant, North Berwick	88	88	176

1889 MUSSELBURGH

Willie Park Jr, Musselburgh	39	39	39	38	155
Andrew Kirkaldy, St Andrews	39	38	39	39	155
(Park won play-off 158 to 163)					
Ben Sayes, North Berwick	39	40	41	39	159
* Johnny Laidlay, Honourable Company	42	39	40	41	162
David Brown, Musselburgh	43	39	41	39	162
Willie Fernie, Troon	45	39	40	40	164

1890 PRESTWICK

* John Ball, Royal Liverpool	82	82	164
Willie Fernie, Troon	85	82	167
Archie Simpson, Carnoustie	85	82	167
Willie Park Jr, Musselburgh	90	80	170
Andrew Kirkaldy, St Andrews	81	89	170
* Horace Hutchinson, Royal North Devon	87	85	172

1891 ST ANDREWS

Hugh Kirkaldy, St Andrews	83	83	166
Willie Fernie, Troon	84	84	168
Andrew Kirkaldy, St Andrews	84	84	168
S. Mure Fergusson, Royal and Ancient	86	84	170
W.D. More, Chester	84	87	171
Willie Park Jr, Musselburgh	88	85	173

(From 1892 the competition was extended to 72 holes)

1892 MUIRFIELD

* Harold Hilton, Royal Liverpool	78	81	72	74	305
* John Ball Jr, Royal Liverpool	75	80	74	79	308
James Kirkaldy, St Andrews	77	83	73	75	308
Sandy Herd, Huddersfield	77	78	77	76	308
J. Kay, Seaton Carew	82	78	74	78	312
Ben Sayers, North Berwick	80	76	81	75	312

1893 PRESTWICK

Willie Auchterlonie, St Andrews	78	81	81	82	322
* Johnny Laidlay, Honourable Company	80	83	80	81	324
Sandy Herd, Huddersfield	82	81	78	84	325
Hugh Kirkaldy, St Andrews	83	79	82	82	326
Andrew Kirkaldy, St Andrews	85	82	82	77	326
J. Kay, Seaton Carew	81	81	80	85	327
R. Simpson, Carnoustie	81	81	80	85	327

1894 SANDWICH

J.H. Taylor, Winchester	84	80	81	81	326
Douglas Rolland, Limpsfield	86	79	84	82	331
Andrew Kirkaldy, St Andrews	86	79	83	84	332
A. Toogood, Eltham	84	85	82	82	333
Willie Fernie, Troon	84	84	86	80	334
Harry Vardon, Bury St Edmunds	86	86	82	80	334
Ben Sayers, North Berwick	85	81	84	84	334

1895 ST ANDREWS

J.H. Taylor, Winchester	86	78	80	78	322
Sandy Herd, Huddersfield	82	77	82	85	326
Andrew Kirkaldy, St Andrews	81	83	84	84	332
G. Pulford, Hoylake	84	81	83	87	335
Archie Simpson, Aberdeen	88	85	78	85	336
Willie Fernie, Troon	86	79	86	86	337
David Brown, Malvern	81	89	83	84	337
David Anderson, Panmure	86	83	84	84	337

1896 MUIRFIELD

Harry Vardon, Ganton	83	78	78	77	316
J.H. Taylor, Winchester	77	78	81	80	316
(Vardon won play-off 157 to 161)					
* Freddie G. Tait, Black Watch	83	75	84	77	319
Willie Fernie, Troon	78	79	82	80	319
Sandy Herd, Huddersfield	72	84	79	85	320
James Braid, Romford	83	81	79	80	323

1897 HOYLAKE

* Harold H. Hilton, Royal Liverpool	80	75	84	75	314
James Braid, Romford	80	74	82	79	315
* Freddie G. Tait, Black Watch	79	79	80	79	317
G. Pulford, Hoylake	80	79	79	79	317
Sandy Herd, Huddersfield	78	81	79	80	318
Harry Vardon, Ganton	84	80	80	76	320

1898 PRESTWICK

Harry Vardon, Ganton	79	75	77	76	307
Willie Park, Musselburgh	76	75	78	79	308
* Harold H. Hilton, Royal Liverpool	76	81	77	75	309
J.H. Taylor, Winchester	78	78	77	79	312
* Freddie G. Tait, Black Watch	81	77	75	82	315
D. Kinnell, Leven	80	77	79	80	316

1899 SANDWICH

Harry Vardon, Ganton	76	76	81	77	310
Jack White, Seaford	79	79	82	75	315
Andrew Kirkaldy, St Andrews	81	79	82	77	319
J.H. Taylor, Mid-Surrey	77	76	83	84	320
James Braid, Romford	78	78	83	84	322
Willie Fernie, Troon	79	83	82	78	322

1900 ST ANDREWS

J.H. Taylor, Mid-Surrey	79	77	78	75	309
Harry Vardon, Ganton	79	81	80	78	317
James Braid, Romford	82	81	80	79	322
Jack White, Seaford	80	81	82	80	323

Willie Auchterlonie, St Andrews	81	85	80	80	326
Willie Park Jr, Musselburgh	80	83	81	84	328

1901 MUIRFIELD

James Braid, Romford	79	76	74	80	309
Harry Vardon, Ganton	77	78	79	78	312
J.H. Taylor, Mid-Surrey	79	83	74	77	313
*Harold H. Hilton, Royal Liverpool	89	80	75	76	320
Sandy Herd, Huddersfield	87	81	81	76	325
Jack White, Seaford	82	82	80	82	326

1902 HOYLAKE

Sandy Herd, Huddersfield	77	76	73	81	307
Harry Vardon, South Herts	72	77	80	79	308
James Braid, Walton Heath	78	76	80	74	308
R. Maxwell, Honourable Company	79	77	79	74	309
Tom Vardon, Ilkley	80	76	78	79	313
J.H. Taylor, Mid-Surrey	81	76	77	80	314
D. Kinnell, Leven	78	80	79	77	314
*Harold H. Hilton, Royal Liverpool	79	76	81	78	314

1903 PRESTWICK

Harry Vardon, South Herts	73	77	72	78	300
Tom Vardon, Ilkley	76	81	75	74	306
Jack White, Sunningdale	77	78	74	79	308
Sandy Herd, Huddersfield	73	83	76	77	309
James Braid, Walton Heath	77	79	79	75	310
R. Thompson, North Berwick	83	78	77	76	314
A.H. Scott, Elie	77	77	83	77	314

1904 SANDWICH

Jack White, Sunningdale	80	75	72	69	296
James Braid, Walton Heath	77	80	69	71	297
J.H. Taylor, Mid-Surrey	77	78	74	68	297
Tom Vardon, Ilkley	77	77	75	72	301
Harry Vardon, South Herts	76	73	79	74	302
James Sherlock, Stoke Poges	83	71	78	77	309

1905 ST ANDREWS

James Braid, Walton Heath	81	78	78	81	318
J.H. Taylor, Mid-Surrey	80	85	78	80	323
R. Jones, Wimbledon Park	81	77	87	78	323
J. Kinnell, Purley Downs	82	79	82	81	324
Arnaud Massy, La Boulie	81	80	82	82	325
E. Gray, Littlehampton	82	81	84	78	325

1906 MUIRFIELD

James Braid, Walton Heath	77	76	74	73	300
J.H. Taylor, Mid-Surrey	77	72	75	80	304
Harry Vardon, South Herts	77	73	77	78	305
*J. Graham Jr, Royal Liverpool	71	79	78	78	306
R. Jones, Wimbledon Park	74	78	73	83	308
Arnaud Massy, La Boulie	76	80	76	78	310

1907 HOYLAKE

Arnaud Massy, La Boulie	76	81	78	77	312
J.H. Taylor, Mid-Surrey	79	79	76	80	314
Tom Vardon, Sandwich	81	81	80	75	317
G. Pulford, Hoylake	81	78	80	78	317
Ted Ray, Ganton	83	80	79	76	318
James Braid, Walton Heath	82	85	75	76	318

1908 PRESTWICK

James Braid, Walton Heath	70	72	77	72	291
Tom Ball, West Lancashire	76	73	76	74	299
Ted Ray, Ganton	79	71	75	76	301
Sandy Herd, Huddersfield	74	74	79	75	302
Harry Vardon, South Herts	79	78	74	75	306
D. Kinnell, Prestwick St Nicholas	75	73	80	78	306

1909 DEAL

J.H. Taylor, Mid-Surrey	74	73	74	74	295
James Braid, Walton Heath	79	73	73	74	299
Tom Ball, West Lancashire	74	75	76	76	301
C. Johns, Southdown	72	76	79	75	302
T.G. Renouf, Manchester	76	78	76	73	303
Ted Ray, Ganton	77	76	76	75	304

1910 ST ANDREWS

James Braid, Walton Heath	76	73	74	76	299
Sandy Herd, Huddersfield	78	74	75	76	303
George Duncan, Hanger Hill	73	77	71	83	304
Laurie Ayton, Bishops Stortford	78	76	75	77	306
Ted Ray, Ganton	76	77	74	81	308
W. Smith, Mexico	77	71	80	80	308
J. Robson, West Surrey	75	80	77	76	308

1911 SANDWICH

Harry Vardon, South Herts	74	74	75	80	303
Arnaud Massy, St Jean de Luz	75	78	74	76	303
(Play-off; Massy conceded at the 35th hole)					
*Harold Hilton, Royal Liverpool	76	74	78	76	304
Sandy Herd, Coombe Hill	77	73	76	78	304
Ted Ray, Ganton	76	72	79	78	305
James Braid, Walton Heath	78	75	74	78	305
J.H. Taylor, Mid-Surrey	72	76	78	79	305

1912 MUIRFIELD

Ted Ray, Oxhey	71	73	76	75	295
Harry Vardon, South Herts	75	72	81	71	299
James Braid, Walton Heath	77	71	77	78	303
George Duncan, Hanger Hill	72	77	78	78	305
Laurie Ayton, Bishops Stortford	74	80	75	79	308
Sandy Herd, Coombe Hill	76	81	76	76	309

1913 HOYLAKE

J.H. Taylor, Mid-Surrey	73	75	77	79	304
Ted Ray, Oxhey	73	74	81	84	312
Harry Vardon, South Herts	79	75	79	80	313
M. Moran, Dollymount	76	74	89	74	313
Johnny J. McDermott, USA	75	80	77	83	315
T.G. Renouf, Manchester	75	78	84	78	315

1914 PRESTWICK

Harry Vardon, South Herts	73	77	78	78	306
J.H. Taylor, Mid-Surrey	74	78	74	83	309
H.B. Simpson, St Annes Old	77	80	78	75	310

Abe Mitchell, Sonning	76	78	79	79	312
Tom Williamson, Notts	75	79	79	79	312
R.G. Wilson, Croham Hurst	76	77	80	80	313

1920 DEAL

George Duncan, Hanger Hill	80	80	71	72	303
Sandy Herd, Coombe Hill	72	81	77	75	305
Ted Ray, Oxhey	72	83	78	73	306
Abe Mitchell, North Foreland	74	73	84	76	307
Len Holland, Northampton	80	78	71	79	308
Jim Barnes, USA	79	74	77	79	309

1921 ST ANDREWS

Jock Hutchison, USA	72	75	79	70	296
*Roger Wethered, Royal and Ancient	78	75	72	71	296
(Hutchison won play-off 150 to 159)					
T. Kerrigan, USA	74	80	72	72	298
Arthur G. Havers, West Lancs	76	74	77	72	299
George Duncan, Hanger Hill	74	75	78	74	301

1922 SANDWICH

Walter Hagen, USA	76	73	79	72	300
George Duncan, Hangar Hill	76	75	81	69	301
Jim Barnes, USA	75	76	77	73	301
Jock Hutchison, USA	79	74	73	76	302
Charles Whitcombe, Dorchester	77	79	72	75	303
J.H. Taylor, Mid-Surrey	73	78	76	77	304

1923 TROON

Arthur G. Havers, Coombe Hill	73	73	73	76	295
Walter Hagen, USA	76	71	74	75	296
Macdonald Smith, USA	80	73	69	75	297
Joe Kirkwood, Australia	72	79	69	78	298
Tom Fernie, Turnberry	73	78	74	75	300
George Duncan, Hanger Hill	79	75	74	74	302
Charles A. Whitcombe, Landsdowne	70	76	74	82	302

1924 HOYLAKE

Walter Hagen, USA	77	73	74	77	301
Ernest Whitcombe, Came Down	77	70	77	78	302
Macdonald Smith, USA	76	74	77	77	304
F. Ball, Langley Park	78	75	74	77	304
J.H. Taylor, Mid-Surrey	75	74	79	79	307
George Duncan, Hanger Hill	74	79	74	81	308
Aubrey Boomer, St Cloud, Paris	75	78	76	79	308

1925 PRESTWICK

Jim Barnes, USA	70	77	79	74	300
Archie Compston, North Manchester	76	75	75	75	301
Ted Ray, Oxhey	77	76	75	73	301
Macdonald Smith, USA	76	69	76	82	303
Abe Mitchell, Unattached	77	76	75	77	305

1926 ROYAL LYTHAM

*Robert T. Jones Jr, USA	72	72	73	74	291
Al Watrous, USA	71	75	69	78	293
Walter Hagen, USA	68	77	74	76	295
George von Elm, USA	75	72	76	72	295
Abe Mitchell, Unattached	78	78	72	71	299
T. Barber, Cavendish	77	73	78	71	299

1927 ST ANDREWS

*Robert T. Jones Jr, USA	68	72	73	72	285
Aubrey Boomer, St Cloud, Paris	76	70	73	72	291
Fred Robson, Cooden Beach	76	72	69	74	291
Joe Kirkwood, Australia	72	72	75	74	293
Ernest Whitcombe, Bournemouth	74	73	73	73	293
Charles Whitcombe, Crews Hill	74	76	71	75	296

1928 SANDWICH

Walter Hagen, USA	75	73	72	72	292
Gene Sarazen, USA	72	76	73	73	294
Archie Compston, Unattached	75	74	73	73	295
Percy Alliss, Berlin	75	76	75	72	298
Fred Robson, Cooden Beach	79	73	73	73	298
Jose Jurado, Argentina	74	71	76	80	301
Aubrey Boomer, St Cloud, Paris	79	73	77	72	301
Jim Barnes, USA	81	73	76	71	301

1929 MUIRFIELD

Walter Hagen, USA	75	67	75	75	292
John Farrell, USA	72	75	76	75	298
Leo Diegel, USA	71	69	82	77	299
Abe Mitchell, St Albans	72	72	78	78	300
Percy Alliss, Berlin	69	76	76	79	300
Bobby Cruickshank, USA	73	74	78	76	301

1930 HOYLAKE

*Robert T. Jones Jr, USA	70	72	74	75	291
Leo Diegel, USA	74	73	71	75	293
Macdonald Smith, USA	70	77	75	71	293
Fred Robson, Cooden Beach	71	72	78	75	296
Horton Smith, USA	72	73	78	73	296
Archie Compston, Coombe Hill	74	73	68	82	297
Jim Barnes, USA	71	77	72	77	297

1931 CARNOUSTIE

Tommy Armour, USA	73	75	77	71	296
Jose Jurado, Argentina	76	71	73	77	297
Percy Alliss, Berlin	74	78	73	73	298
Gene Sarazen, USA	74	76	75	73	298
Macdonald Smith, USA	75	77	71	76	299
John Farrell, USA	72	77	75	75	299

1932 PRINCE'S

Gene Sarazen, USA	70	69	70	74	283
Macdonald Smith, USA	71	76	71	70	288
Arthur G. Havers, Sandy Lodge	74	71	68	76	289
Charles Whitcombe, Crews Hill	71	73	73	75	292
Percy Alliss, Beaconsfield	71	71	78	72	292
Alf Padgham, Royal Ashdown Forest	76	72	74	70	292

1933 ST ANDREWS

Densmore Shute, USA	73	73	73	73	292
Craig Wood, USA	77	72	68	75	292
(Shute won play-off 149 to 154)					
Sid Easterbrook, Knowle	73	72	71	77	293
Gene Sarazen, USA	72	73	73	75	293
Leo Diegel, USA	75	70	71	77	293
Olin Dutra, USA	76	76	70	72	294

1934 SANDWICH

Henry Cotton, Waterloo, Belgium	67	65	72	79	283
Sid Brews, South Africa	76	71	70	71	288
Alf Padgham, Sundridge Park	71	70	75	74	290
Macdonald Smith, USA	77	71	72	72	292
Joe Kirkwood, USA	74	69	71	78	292
Marcel Dallemagne, France	71	73	71	77	292

1935 MUIRFIELD

Alf Perry, Leatherhead	69	75	67	72	283
Alf Padgham, Sundridge Park	70	72	74	71	287
Charles Whitcombe, Crews Hill	71	68	73	76	288
Bert Gadd, Brand Hall	72	75	71	71	289
Lawson Little, USA	75	71	74	69	289
Henry Picard, USA	72	73	72	75	292

1936 HOYLAKE

Alf Padgham, Sundridge Park	73	72	71	71	287
Jimmy Adams, Romford	71	73	71	73	288
Henry Cotton, Waterloo, Belgium	73	72	70	74	289
Marcel Dallemagne, France	73	72	75	69	289
Percy Alliss, Leeds Municipal	74	72	74	71	291
T. Green, Burnham Beeches	74	72	70	75	291
Gene Sarazen, USA	73	75	70	73	291

1937 CARNOUSTIE

Henry Cotton, Ashridge	74	72	73	71	290
Reg Whitcombe, Parkstone	72	70	74	76	292
Charles Lacey, USA	76	75	70	72	293
Charles Whitcombe, Crews Hill	73	71	74	76	294
Bryon Nelson, USA	75	76	71	74	296
Ed Dudley, USA	70	74	78	75	297

1938 SANDWICH

Reg Whitcombe, Parkstone	71	71	75	78	295
Jimmy Adams, Royal Liverpool	70	71	78	78	297
Henry Cotton, Ashridge	74	73	77	74	298
Alf Padgham, Sundridge Park	74	72	75	82	303
Jack Busson, Pannal	71	69	83	80	303
Richard Burton, Sale	71	69	78	85	303
Allan Dailey, Wanstead	73	72	80	78	303

1939 ST ANDREWS

Richard Burton, Sale	70	72	77	71	290
Johnny Bulla, USA	77	71	71	73	292
Johnny Fallon, Huddersfield	71	73	71	79	294
Bill Shankland, Temple Newsam	72	73	72	77	294
Alf Perry, Leatherhead	71	74	73	76	294
Reg Whitcombe, Parkstone	71	75	74	74	294
Sam King, Knole Park	74	72	75	73	294

1946 ST ANDREWS

Sam Snead, USA	71	70	74	75	290
Bobby Locke, South Africa	69	74	75	76	294
Johnny Bulla, USA	71	72	72	79	294
Charlie Ward, Little Aston	73	73	73	76	295
Henry Cotton, Royal Mid-Surrey	70	70	76	79	295
Dai Rees, Hindhead	75	67	73	80	295
Norman von Nida, Australia	70	76	74	75	295

1947 HOYLAKE

Fred Daly, Balmoral, Belfast	73	70	78	72	293
Reg Horne, Hendon	77	74	72	71	294
*Frank Stranahan, USA	71	79	72	72	294
Bill Shankland, Temple Newsam	76	74	75	70	295
Richard Burton, Coombe Hill	77	71	77	71	296
Charlie Ward, Little Aston	76	73	76	72	297
Sam King, Wildernesse	75	72	77	73	297
Arthur Lees, Dore and Totley	75	74	72	76	297
Johnny Bulla, USA	80	72	74	71	297
Henry Cotton, Royal Mid-Surrey	69	78	74	76	297
Norman von Nida, Australia	74	76	71	76	297

1948 MUIRFIELD

Henry Cotton, Royal Mid-Surrey	71	66	75	72	284
Fred Daly, Balmoral, Belfast	72	71	73	73	289
Norman von Nida, Australia	71	72	76	71	290
Roberto de Vicenzo, Argentina	70	73	72	75	290
Jack Hargreaves, Sutton Coldfield	76	68	73	73	290
Charlie Ward, Little Aston	69	72	75	74	290

1949 SANDWICH

Bobby Locke, South Africa	69	76	68	70	283
Harry Bradshaw, Kilcroney, Eire	68	77	68	70	283
(Locke won play-off 135 to 147)					
Roberto de Vicenzo, Argentina	68	75	73	69	285
Sam King, Knole Park	71	69	74	72	286
Charlie Ward, Little Aston	73	71	70	72	286
Arthur Lees, Dore and Totley	74	70	72	71	287
Max Faulkner, Royal Mid-Surrey	71	71	71	74	287

1950 TROON

Bobby Locke, South Africa	69	72	70	68	279
Roberto de Vicenzo, Argentina	72	71	68	70	281
Fred Daly, Balmoral, Belfast	75	72	69	66	282
Dai Rees, South Herts	71	68	72	71	282
E. Moore, South Africa	74	68	73	68	283
Max Faulkner, Royal Mid-Surrey	73	70	70	71	283

1951 ROYAL PORTRUSH

Max Faulkner, Unattached	71	70	70	74	285
Tony Cerda, Argentina	74	72	71	70	287
Charlie Ward, Little Aston	75	73	74	68	290
Fred Daly, Balmoral, Belfast	74	70	75	73	292
Jimmy Adams, Wentworth	68	77	75	72	292
Bobby Locke, South Africa	71	74	74	74	293

Bill Shankland, Temple Newsam	73	76	72	72	293
Norman Sutton, Leigh	73	70	74	76	293
Harry Weetman, Croham Hurst	73	71	75	74	293
Peter Thomson, Australia	70	75	73	75	293

1952 ROYAL LYTHAM

Bobby Locke, South Africa	69	71	74	73	287
Peter Thomson, Australia	68	73	77	70	288
Fred Daly, Balmoral, Belfast	67	69	77	76	289
Henry Cotton, Royal Mid-Surrey	75	74	74	71	294
Tony Cerda, Argentina	73	73	76	73	295
Sam King, Knole Park	71	74	74	76	295

1953 CARNOUSTIE

Ben Hogan, USA	73	71	70	68	282
*Frank Stranahan, USA	70	74	73	69	286
Dai Rees, South Herts	72	70	73	71	286
Peter Thomson, Australia	72	72	71	71	286
Tony Cerda, Argentina	75	71	69	71	286
Roberto de Vicenzo, Argentina	72	71	71	73	287

1954 ROYAL BIRKDALE

Peter Thomson, Australia	72	71	69	71	283
Sid Scott, Carlisle City	76	67	69	72	284
Dai Rees, South Herts	72	71	69	72	284
Bobby Locke, South Africa	74	71	69	70	284
Jimmy Adams, Royal Mid-Surrey	73	75	69	69	286
Tony Cerda, Argentina	71	71	73	71	286
J. Turnesa, USA	72	72	71	71	286

1955 ST ANDREWS

Peter Thomson, Australia	71	68	70	72	281
Johnny Fallon, Huddersfield	73	67	73	70	283
Frank Jowle, Edgbaston	70	71	69	74	284
Bobby Locke, South Africa	74	69	70	72	285
Tony Cerda, Argentina	73	71	71	71	286
Ken Bousfield, Coombe Hill	71	75	70	70	286
Harry Weetman, Croham Hurst	71	71	70	74	286
Bernard Hunt, Hartsbourne	70	71	74	71	286
Flory van Donck, Belgium	71	72	71	72	286

1956 HOYLAKE

Peter Thomson, Australia	70	70	72	74	286
Flory van Donck, Belgium	71	74	70	74	289
Roberto de Vicenzo, Argentina	71	70	79	70	290
Gary Player, South Africa	71	76	73	71	291
John Panton, Glenbervie	74	76	72	70	292
Henry Cotton, Temple	72	76	71	74	293
E. Bertolino, Argentina	69	72	76	76	293

1957 ST ANDREWS

Bobby Locke, South Africa	69	72	68	70	279
Peter Thomson, Australia	73	69	70	70	282
Eric Brown, Buchanan Castle	67	72	73	71	283
Angel Miguel, Spain	72	72	69	72	285
David Thomas, Sudbury	72	74	70	70	286
Tom Haliburton, Wentworth	72	73	68	73	286
*Dick Smith, Prestwick	71	72	72	71	286
Flory van Donck, Belgium	72	68	74	72	286

1958 ROYAL LYTHAM

Peter Thomson, Australia	66	72	67	73	278
David Thomas, Sudbury	70	68	69	71	278
(Thomson won play-off 139 to 143)					
Eric Brown, Buchanan Castle	73	70	65	71	279
Christy O'Connor, Killarney	67	68	73	71	279
Flory van Donck, Belgium	70	70	67	74	281
Leopoldo Ruiz, Argentina	71	65	72	73	281

1959 MUIRFIELD

Gary Player, South Africa	75	71	70	68	284
Flory van Donck, Belgium	70	70	73	73	286
Fred Bullock, Prestwick St Ninians	68	70	74	74	286
Sid Scott, Roehampton	73	70	73	71	287
Christy O'Connor, Royal Dublin	73	74	72	69	288
* Reid Jack, Dullatur	71	75	68	74	288
Sam King, Knole Park	70	74	68	76	288
John Panton, Glenbervie	72	72	71	73	288

1960 ST ANDREWS

Kel Nagle, Australia	69	67	71	71	278
Arnold Palmer, USA	70	71	70	68	279
Bernard Hunt, Hartsbourne	72	73	71	66	282
Harold Henning, South Africa	72	72	69	69	282
Roberto de Vicenzo, Argentina	67	67	75	73	282
* Guy Wolstenholme, Sunningdale	74	70	71	68	283

1961 ROYAL BIRKDALE

Arnold Palmer, USA	70	73	69	72	284
Dai Rees, South Herts	68	74	71	72	285
Christy O'Connor, Royal Dublin	71	77	67	73	288
Neil Coles, Coombe Hill	70	77	69	72	288
Eric Brown, Unattached	73	76	70	70	289
Kel Nagle, Australia	68	75	75	71	289

1962 TROON

Arnold Palmer, USA	71	69	67	69	276
Kel Nagle, Australia	71	71	70	70	282
Brian Huggett, Romford	75	71	74	69	289
Phil Rodgers, USA	75	70	72	72	289
Bob Charles, NZ	75	70	70	75	290
Sam Snead, USA	76	73	72	71	292
Peter Thomson, Australia	70	77	75	70	292

1963 ROYAL LYTHAM

Bob Charles, NZ	68	72	66	71	277
Phil Rodgers, USA	67	68	73	69	277
(Charles won play-off 140 to 148)					
Jack Nicklaus, USA	71	67	70	70	278
Kel Nagle, Australia	69	70	73	71	283
Peter Thomson, Australia	67	69	71	78	285
Christy O'Connor, Royal Dublin	74	68	76	68	286

1964 ST ANDREWS

Tony Lema, USA	73	68	68	70	279
Jack Nicklaus, USA	76	74	66	68	284
Roberto de Vicenzo, Argentina	76	72	70	67	285

Bernard Hunt, Hartsbourne	73	74	70	70	287
Bruce Devlin, Australia	72	72	73	73	290
Christy O'Connor, Royal Dublin	71	73	74	73	291
Harry Weetman, Selsdon Park	72	71	75	73	291

1965 ROYAL BIRKDALE

Peter Thomson, Australia	74	68	72	71	285
Christy O'Connor, Royal Dublin	69	73	74	71	287
Brian Huggett, Romford	73	68	76	70	287
Roberto de Vicenzo, Argentina	74	69	73	72	288
Kel Nagle, Australia	74	70	73	72	289
Tony Lema, USA	68	72	75	74	289
Bernard Hunt, Hartsbourne	74	74	70	71	289

1966 MUIRFIELD

Jack Nicklaus, USA	70	67	75	70	282
David Thomas, Dunham Forest	72	73	69	69	283
Doug Sanders, USA	71	70	72	70	283
Gary Player, South Africa	72	74	71	69	286
Bruce Devlin, Australia	73	69	74	70	286
Kel Nagle, Australia	72	68	76	70	286
Phil Rodgers, USA	74	66	70	76	286

1967 HOYLAKE

Roberto de Vicenzo, Argentina	70	71	67	70	278
Jack Nicklaus, USA	71	69	71	69	280
Clive Clark, Sunningdale	70	73	69	72	284
Gary Player, South Africa	72	71	67	74	284
Tony Jacklin, Potters Bar	73	69	73	70	285
Sebastian Miguel, Spain	72	74	68	72	286
Harold Henning, South Africa	74	70	71	71	286

1968 CARNOUSTIE

Gary Player, South Africa	74	71	71	73	289
Jack Nicklaus, USA	76	69	73	73	291
Bob Charles, NZ	72	72	71	76	291
Billy Casper, USA	72	68	74	78	292
Maurice Bembridge, Little Aston	71	75	73	74	293
Brian Barnes, Burnham & Berrow	70	74	80	71	295
Neil Coles, Coombe Hill	75	76	71	73	295
Gay Brewer, USA	74	73	72	76	295

1969 ROYAL LYTHAM

Tony Jacklin, Potters Bar	68	70	70	72	280
Bob Charles, NZ	66	69	75	72	282
Peter Thomson, Australia	71	70	70	72	283
Roberto de Vicenzo, Argentina	72	73	66	72	283
Christy O'Connor, Royal Dublin	71	65	74	74	284
Jack Nicklaus, USA	75	70	68	72	285
Davis Love Jr, USA	70	73	71	71	285

1970 ST ANDREWS

Jack Nicklaus, USA	68	69	73	73	283
Doug Sanders, USA	68	71	71	73	283
(Nicklaus won play-off 72 to 73)					
Harold Henning, South Africa	67	72	73	73	285
Lee Trevino, USA	68	68	72	77	285
Tony Jacklin, Potters Bar	67	70	73	76	286
Neil Coles, Coombe Hill	65	74	72	76	287
Peter Oosterhuis, Dulwich and Sydenham	73	69	69	76	287

1971 ROYAL BIRKDALE

Lee Trevino, USA	69	70	69	70	278
Lu Liang Huan, Taiwan	70	70	69	70	279
Tony Jacklin, Potters Bar	69	70	70	71	280
Craig de Foy, Coombe Hill	72	72	68	69	281
Jack Nicklaus, USA	71	71	72	69	283
Charles Coody, USA	74	71	70	68	283

1972 MUIRFIELD

Lee Trevino, USA	71	70	66	71	278
Jack Nicklaus, USA	70	72	71	66	279
Tony Jacklin, Potters Bar	69	72	67	72	280
Doug Sanders, USA	71	71	69	70	281
Brian Barnes, Fairway DR	71	72	69	71	283
Gary Player, South Africa	71	71	76	67	285

1973 TROON

Tom Weiskopf, USA	68	67	71	70	276
Neil Coles, Holiday Inns	71	72	70	66	279
Johnny Miller, USA	70	68	69	72	279
Jack Nicklaus, USA	69	70	76	65	280
Bert Yancey, USA	69	69	73	70	281
Peter Butler, Golf Domes	71	72	74	69	286

1974 ROYAL LYTHAM

Gary Player, South Africa	69	68	75	70	282
Peter Oosterhuis, Pacific Harbour	71	71	73	71	286
Jack Nicklaus, USA	74	72	70	71	287
Hubert Green, USA	71	74	72	71	288
Danny Edwards, USA	70	73	76	73	292
Lu Liang Huan, Taiwan	72	72	75	73	292

1975 CARNOUSTIE

Tom Watson, USA	71	67	69	72	279
Jack Newton, Australia	69	71	65	74	279
(Watson won play-off 71 to 72)					
Bobby Cole, South Africa	72	66	66	76	280
Jack Nicklaus, USA	69	71	68	72	280
Johnny Miller, USA	71	69	66	74	280
Graham Marsh, Australia	72	67	71	71	281

1976 ROYAL BIRKDALE

Johnny Miller, USA	72	68	73	66	279
Jack Nicklaus, USA	74	70	72	69	285
Severiano Ballesteros, Spain	69	69	73	74	285
Raymond Floyd, USA	76	67	73	70	286
Mark James, Burghley Park	76	72	74	66	288
Hubert Green, USA	72	70	78	68	288
Christy O'Connor Jr, Shannon	69	73	75	71	288
Tom Kite, USA	70	74	73	71	288
Tommy Horton, Royal Jersey	74	69	72	73	288

1977 TURNBERRY

Tom Watson, USA	68	70	65	65	268
Jack Nicklaus, USA	68	70	65	66	269

Hubert Green, USA	72	66	74	67	279
Lee Trevino, USA	68	70	72	70	280
Ben Crenshaw, USA	71	69	66	75	281
George Burns, USA	70	70	72	69	281

1978 ST ANDREWS

Jack Nicklaus, USA	71	72	69	69	281
Simon Owen, NZ	70	75	67	71	283
Ben Crenshaw, USA	70	69	73	71	283
Raymond Floyd, USA	69	75	71	68	283
Tom Kite, USA	72	69	72	70	283
Peter Oosterhuis, GB	72	70	69	73	284

1979 ROYAL LYTHAM

Severiano Ballesteros, Spain	73	65	75	70	283
Jack Nicklaus, USA	72	69	73	72	286
Ben Crenshaw, USA	72	71	72	71	286
Mark James, Burghley Park	76	69	69	73	287
Rodger Davis, Australia	75	70	70	73	288
Hale Irwin, USA	68	68	75	78	289

1980 MUIRFIELD

Tom Watson, USA	68	70	64	69	271
Lee Trevino, USA	68	67	71	69	275
Ben Crenshaw, USA	70	70	68	69	277
Jack Nicklaus, USA	73	67	71	69	280
Carl Mason, Unattached	72	69	70	69	280

1981 SANDWICH

Bill Rogers, USA	72	66	67	71	276
Bernhard Langer, Germany	73	67	70	70	280
Mark James, Otley	72	70	68	73	283
Raymond Floyd, USA	74	70	69	70	283
Sam Torrance, Caledonian Hotel	72	69	73	70	284
Bruce Leitzke, USA	76	69	71	69	285
Manuel Pinero, Spain	73	74	68	70	285

1982 TROON

Tom Watson, USA	69	71	74	70	284
Peter Oosterhuis, GB	74	67	74	70	285
Nick Price, South Africa	69	69	74	73	285
Nick Faldo, Glynwed Ltd	73	73	71	69	286
Des Smyth, EAL Tubes	70	69	74	73	286
Tom Purtzer, USA	76	66	75	69	286
Massy Kuramoto, Japan	71	73	71	71	286

1983 ROYAL BIRKDALE

Tom Watson, USA	67	68	70	70	275
Hale Irwin, USA	69	68	72	67	276
Andy Bean, USA	70	69	70	67	276
Graham Marsh, Australia	69	70	74	64	277
Lee Trevino, USA	69	66	73	70	278
Severiano Ballesteros, Spain	71	71	69	68	279
Harold Henning, South Africa	71	69	70	69	279

1984 ST ANDREWS

Severiano Ballesteros, Spain	69	68	70	69	276
Bernhard Langer, Germany	71	68	68	71	278
Tom Watson, USA	71	68	66	73	278
Fred Couples, USA	70	69	74	68	281
Lanny Wadkins, USA	70	69	73	69	281
Greg Norman, Australia	67	74	74	67	282
Nick Faldo, Glynwed Int.	69	68	76	69	282

1985 SANDWICH

Sandy Lyle, Scotland	68	71	73	70	282
Payne Stewart, USA	70	75	70	68	283
Jose Rivero, Spain	74	72	70	68	284
Christy O'Connor Jr, Ireland	64	76	72	72	284
Mark O'Meara, USA	70	72	70	72	284
David Graham, Australia	68	71	70	75	284
Bernhard Langer, Germany	72	69	68	75	284

1986 TURNBERRY

Greg Norman, Australia	74	63	74	69	280
Gordon J. Brand, England	71	68	75	71	285
Bernhard Langer, Germany	72	70	76	68	286
Ian Woosnam, Wales	70	74	70	72	286
Nick Faldo, England	71	70	76	70	287

1987 MUIRFIELD

Nick Faldo, England	68	69	71	71	279
Rodger Davis, Australia	64	73	74	69	280
Paul Azinger, USA	68	68	71	73	280
Ben Crenshaw, USA	73	68	72	68	281
Payne Stewart, USA	71	66	72	72	281
David Frost, South Africa	70	68	70	74	282
Tom Watson, USA	69	69	71	74	283

1988 ROYAL LYTHAM

Severiano Ballesteros, Spain	67	71	70	65	273
Nick Price, Zimbabwe	70	67	69	69	275
Nick Faldo, England	71	69	68	71	279
Fred Couples, USA	73	69	71	68	281
Gary Koch, USA	71	72	70	68	281
Peter Senior, Australia	70	73	70	69	282

1989 ROYAL TROON

Mark Calcavecchia, USA	71	68	68	68	275
Greg Norman, Australia	69	70	72	64	275
Wayne Grady, Australia	68	67	69	71	275
(Calcavecchia won four-hole play-off)					
Tom Watson, USA	69	68	68	72	277
Jodie Mudd, USA	73	67	68	70	278

1990 ST ANDREWS

Nick Faldo, England	67	65	67	71	270
Mark McNulty, Zimbabwe	74	68	68	65	275
Payne Stewart, USA	68	68	68	71	275
Jodie Mudd, USA	72	66	72	66	276
Ian Woosnam, Wales	68	69	70	69	276

FINAL RESULTS

HOLE		1	2	3	4	5	6	7	8	9	10	11	12	13	14	15	16	17	18	
PAR		4	4	4	3	4	4	3	4	4	4	4	3	4	3	5	4	5	4	TOTAL
Ian Baker-Finch	Round 1	4	5	4	3	4	4	3	4	3	4	4	4	5	3	6	4	4	3	71
	Round 2	4	5	4	4	4	5	3	4	3	4	4	3	4	3	5	4	4	4	71
	Round 3	4	3	3	3	3	4	4	4	4	3	4	3	3	4	5	4	3	3	64
	Round 4	4	3	3	2	4	3	2	4	4	5	4	3	4	3	5	4	4	5	66-272
Mike Harwood	Round 1	4	3	4	2	4	5	3	3	4	3	4	3	4	3	5	4	5	5	68
	Round 2	5	3	4	3	4	5	3	4	4	4	4	2	4	3	5	5	4	4	70
	Round 3	4	5	4	3	4	3	3	4	5	4	5	4	3	2	5	3	4	4	69
	Round 4	4	4	4	3	4	5	3	3	3	4	3	3	4	3	5	3	5	4	67-274
Fred Couples	Round 1	3	5	5	3	4	4	3	3	4	4	5	3	4	3	5	4	4	6	72
	Round 2	4	5	4	3	4	5	3	4	4	4	4	3	4	2	5	4	3	4	69
	Round 3	5	3	4	4	4	5	3	3	3	4	4	3	4	4	5	4	5	3	70
	Round 4	4	4	3	3	3	5	3	3	4	3	3	2	3	3	5	4	5	4	64-275
Mark O'Meara	Round 1	3	4	3	2	4	5	4	4	5	5	4	4	4	3	5	4	5	3	71
	Round 2	4	4	4	3	5	4	3	4	3	5	4	3	4	4	5	3	3	3	68
	Round 3	4	5	4	3	4	5	2	4	4	4	4	2	4	3	4	5	3	3	67
	Round 4	4	4	4	4	4	4	2	5	4	4	4	3	4	3	4	4	4	4	69-275
Jodie Mudd	Round 1	3	5	4	3	3	5	3	4	5	4	4	3	4	3	5	4	6	4	72
	Round 2	4	3	4	2	5	5	2	5	4	4	4	3	4	3	6	4	4	4	70
	Round 3	5	4	4	2	5	4	3	4	4	4	3	3	4	3	5	5	5	5	72
	Round 4	4	4	3	3	3	5	2	4	4	3	3	3	3	3	4	4	4	4	63-277
Bob Tway	Round 1	4	5	4	3	4	5	3	4	5	4	5	3	4	4	5	5	4	4	75
	Round 2	4	6	3	3	4	4	2	2	4	3	4	2	4	3	5	4	5	4	66
	Round 3	5	3	4	3	3	5	3	5	4	3	4	3	3	3	6	5	4	4	70
	Round 4	5	3	3	3	4	4	3	4	3	3	4	3	4	3	4	4	5	4	66-277
Eamonn Darcy	Round 1	4	4	4	3	4	5	3	5	4	4	4	3	4	3	5	5	4	5	73
	Round 2	5	4	4	3	4	4	3	3	4	5	3	3	3	3	5	4	4	4	68
	Round 3	3	4	4	3	3	3	3	3	5	4	4	2	5	3	4	4	5	4	66
	Round 4	4	4	4	2	4	5	3	3	3	4	4	3	4	4	7	4	4	4	70-277
Craig Parry	Round 1	4	4	3	3	4	4	3	4	5	4	4	3	4	3	5	5	5	4	71
	Round 2	4	5	3	3	3	5	3	3	4	5	4	3	4	2	5	5	5	4	70
	Round 3	5	4	4	2	4	4	3	4	4	4	4	3	4	3	4	5	4	4	69
	Round 4	3	4	3	3	4	5	4	3	5	4	4	4	4	2	5	4	4	3	68-278
Greg Norman	Round 1	4	6	4	3	4	5	2	4	4	4	4	4	4	3	5	5	4	5	74
	Round 2	4	3	3	4	4	4	2	4	4	5	4	3	4	3	5	4	4	4	68
	Round 3	5	5	4	3	4	4	3	4	3	3	4	4	5	3	5	4	4	4	71
	Round 4	4	3	4	2	3	4	3	5	5	3	4	3	4	2	4	3	5	5	66-279
Bernhard Langer	Round 1	3	4	4	4	4	5	4	3	4	4	4	3	5	3	4	4	5	4	71
	Round 2	5	4	5	3	3	4	3	4	4	3	4	4	5	3	5	5	3	4	71
	Round 3	4	4	4	3	3	4	3	4	5	4	4	3	4	4	5	4	4	4	70
	Round 4	4	3	4	3	3	5	2	4	4	4	5	3	3	4	4	4	4	4	67-279
Seve Ballesteros	Round 1	4	4	4	3	3	4	3	4	4	3	4	3	5	2	6	4	3	3	66
	Round 2	5	5	4	3	4	5	3	4	3	4	4	3	4	3	5	5	5	4	73
	Round 3	4	4	4	4	5	4	3	3	4	4	4	2	4	3	5	4	4	4	69
	Round 4	5	4	5	3	4	4	2	4	4	4	4	3	4	3	4	5	5	4	71-279

Scenes from the sidelines of the Open Championship.

Bowring
Insurance Brokers
WELCOME TO THE 120th. OPEN CHAMPIONSHIP
Bowring
Insurance Brokers

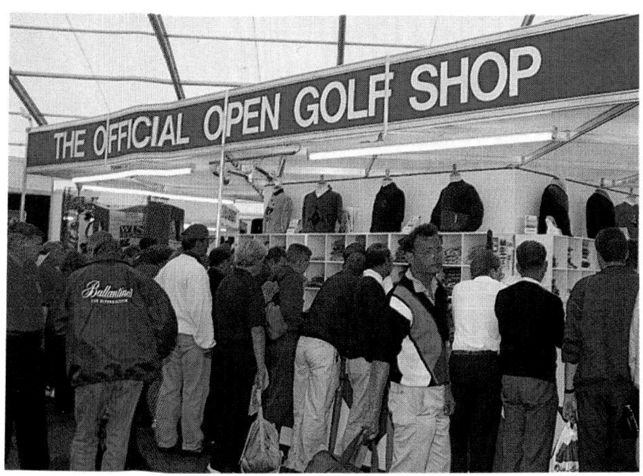
THE OFFICIAL OPEN GOLF SHOP
Ballantine's

Plaque
Practice
Ground
Putting
Green
Clubhouse